Jesus

Burden

Bearer

365 Day Prayer Book

Ron P. Wallace

Burkhart Books
Bedford, TX
www.burkhartbooks.com

Dedication

  This prayer book is dedicated to those whose daily walk in life takes you through those lonesome valleys alone. Even those closest to you can't identify with your dark valleys and dark nights of the soul. They don't have any answers, so they choose to leave you alone and say nothing.

  I am also a fellow traveler who has encountered those same valleys and dark nights. I walk them by myself, but recognize Jesus is there by my side. There is no burden too great that He cannot help us. There is no valley so deep that He will leave us. There is no night so dark that He will lose us.

  These prayers were prayed and written to Jesus. Read them aloud the next time you try to pray, but don't know what to say. He sees you. He also hears you. But most of all, He is there for you to cast your burden upon Him.

  After all that is said and done, Jesus will always be there as the burden bearer. Nothing else then needs to be said or done.

January 1

Jesus, You brought healing to so many who came to You. I come to You this day and ask that You touch my eyes to see life from Your perspective. Touch my ears to hear what You are saying to me. Touch my mind and make it whole. Bring life to those areas that don't seem to function properly. Bring a balance to what is not in balance. But most of all, touch my heart where only You can make a difference. The world has been changed because of You. Change me to become like You.

January 2

Jesus, there are things You choose not to reveal to me. Thank You for that kind of love and protection. I sometimes ask for a revelation and You remain silent. I may not understand, but You know why You chose to do so. Help me to understand what You do make known. Help me to trust You in all things, both the seen and the unseen.

January 3

Jesus, You made a way for me to experience the love of a heavenly Father. I know it's there, but sometimes I don't feel it. Make this day one where I can feel that love wrapped around me in a tender and loving way. I need it in a special way today like I've never known before.

January 4

Jesus, when I seek You, I seek the truth to my questions in life. My misunderstandings cause me to take missteps. Order my steps in a way that bring revelation to the situation and give direction to where You are taking me. I don't want to wander, but to see the wonder of Your grace that is so amazing.

January 5

Jesus, when I lay down at night, my thoughts become questions. Why did certain things happen and why did I respond in a particular way? Sometimes I feel as if no answers will ever be given to my questions. If I can't get answers, then give me the assurance of Your love. Help me to love myself in a way You love me.

January 6

Jesus, help me to count all things as joy. I sometimes lose sight of Your purpose and the joy of my salvation. I must be all about You for others to want what I have in You. It's not about what I want, but what You desire for me. Help me to desire all that You want me to have and not what I want for myself.

January 7

Jesus, I am to have life in You. The Spirit of God is in me because of what You did for me. That is all I need. People look for more in life, but I want to look more for You while living this life. You were not defeated on the cross and I don't want to be defeated while I follow You with my cross. Give me the strength to take life one day at a time.

January 8

Jesus, You died for me, yet I don't live for You the way You want me to live. I sometimes want to give up, but You never gave up on me. And You never will. Help me to hold on and not give up on You or myself.

January 9

Jesus, no one can love me the way You do. You showed me by dying for me. Help me to experience Your love and live my life in a way that pleases You. Help me to live fully alive as Your presence lives in me.

January 10

Jesus, You don't want me to be lonely or experience loneliness as a way of life. But that seems to be the way I have spent so much of my life. Days seem shorter as my life span continues to shorten. I know this is the day You made for me. Show me the way as You make a way for me today.

January 11

Jesus, You experienced disappointment in some of those closest to You. Many are disappointed in me. They would never say it to my face, but I can see it on their faces. It's not about pleasing them, but pleasing You. Help me to keep You on my mind in the way I was on Your mind when You died for me.

January 12

Jesus, You know all about my troubles. You knew when they began, but more importantly, You know when they will end. I pray You will help me make it until then. Thank You for giving me the strength to make it to this point. I know You will see me home. Help me to sense Your presence the remainder of the way.

January 13

Jesus, You said to "Follow Me." I tried to do the best I could from the beginning. My life has never been the same, but still not what it needs to be for You to complete Your work in me. Let my thoughts be flooded with waves of mercy. I bow before You with a heart full of gratitude. My lips shall praise You for the life You give me today. Let this day be all about You.

January 14

Jesus, You called me to Your side. You said You would never leave me, but I wandered away at times. Doubts caused a divide that made me doubt Your true identity. I give You reasons to doubt me, but You never move away from me. Draw me closer to Your side that was pierced for me. Let me feel Your love so I can have hope once again.

January 15

Jesus, You made it clear You are the only way to the Father. You showed us the way through your life and death. You now live forever, and I should have no fear of death. You conquered death, so help me to conquer my fear of dying and my life having little meaning. You are the reason for a continuous meaning beyond this life.

January 16

Jesus, I need You this very hour. What is life tomorrow if I live today for any other reason except for You? I know You are here with me because You told me so. Reveal more of Yourself today so I can let others see more of You in me today.

January 17

Jesus, You are in my thoughts at times, even though I don't

think about You all the time. I become self centered in my thinking and think life should go more my way. Help me to know more of who I am by living more for You this day. Make me Your instrument of praise because of what You did for me so I can be about You in all that I do.

January 18

Jesus, thank You for what You do through me in spite of the way I sometimes think about myself. You bring others to life when they see You living in me and through me. I want to decrease more so the work You want to do in me will increase. You are the Blessed Hope and I want to encourage and bring hope to others because of You.

January 19

Jesus, You spoke of your peace that was to remain on earth. Your peace can bring calmness to any storm and peace to the war raging in me. I have You in my heart, but I need Your peace in my soul. Bring calmness and stillness to my being. Have Your way and help me relinquish my own strongholds.

January 20

Jesus, You are my fortress that no one can take over or overrun. You gave Your word that the enemy flees at Your presence. You are in me. I stand in need of You. Help me this day to see myself as a victorious warrior whose enemy was defeated at Calvary. You died for me then. I know You are with me now.

January 21

Jesus, You gave Your all for me. All I wanted in life was to live for You. Life didn't take me where I thought I would go. It has been a journey of uncertainty and sometimes without specific direction. But I trusted You just the same. I can truly say I did my best to follow You. I have been blessed, but believe the best is yet to come. I want to live with that hope until the day I die. Help me not to give up when others sometime give up on me.

January 22

Jesus, You are the Son of God. I am a child of God. You fulfilled Your Father's will for Your life. I am still living and have yet to fulfill it to completion. I have hope each day that more of Your will shall be revealed. The challenge of living faces me each day. I sometimes don't understand life's meaning. Keep me wrapped in Your protection and Your love as I try to make this day count for You.

January 23

Jesus, how can You love me the way You do? I want to love You more because there is so much more of You to be loved. You forgave when You were forsaken by others. I sometimes want to run away from life, but I know I will end up running into Your love. I want to live what life I have left for You. I leave my future in Your hands. Help me to live for the present in Your presence. Let me see You so others can see You in me.

January 24

Jesus, You are as much with me today as the day You became my Savior and Lord. You give me every reason to trust You, but my trust falls short so many times. I don't know why You continue to trust me as I fall so short of the mark and don't fully trust You. You have never given me a reason not to trust You. Once again I ask for Your forgiveness and I want so much to please You.

And without faith, it is impossible to please You.

January 25

Jesus, You showed me how to live life to its fullest by the way You lived Your life. You came to give me life abundantly, one that can overflow with blessings You have for me. The enemy tries to have those blessings withheld by me not releasing my faith. I want Your blessings and You only ask for a simple faith in return. I believe, Jesus. Help my unbelief.

January 26

Jesus, come quickly to my rescue. The hounds of fear continually bark in my mind, trying to drive me into a denial of Your power. They run in fear when You are near. Allow me to draw close to Your side. I desperately need You and so much want victory to be gained in my life.

January 27

Jesus, You lived on earth before You died. Help me to live a life pleasing to You before I die here on earth. You know how I am to live and You showed me the way. Help me to live for You that I know can only come from You. You made a way. Help me to show others the way to You by living a life that pleases You.

January 28

Jesus, I should never question Your love, but I do question the life I have lived while living. I know Your ways are not my ways. I never want my way, but the life You set before me. You know where You will take me and how it will end. I want to be faithful to the end.

January 29

Jesus, no one knows me better than You. I wish I knew myself better so I could better understand myself. You know my ways, even when I don't know where life is taking me. I know certain things don't need to be made known. I desire a glimpse of Your glory and an assurance that Your plan in my life is being fulfilled.

January 30

Jesus, You calmed the sea by addressing the invisible wind that brought about the turbulence. A storm rages inside of me that is unseen by others. I feel it crashing against my inner being. Speak stillness to my condition. Bring calm to my spirit. Let the dawn break the dark night of my soul so I can see Your hand on my life.

January 31

Jesus, You wept and agonized while living here. You are able to see each tear shed and hear the silent groans deep within my soul. I tell You of troubles You already know. I don't yet know the way to go. It is in Your time that You will show me. I turn to no one but You because there is no one but You that can help me. Remember my faithfulness and move me to the land You promised for those who try to remain faithful during these trying times.

February 1

Jesus, You are my hope, the only hope I have. Others may forsake me, but You forgive me. Thank You for the tender mercies You send my way. They endure forever and cover a multitude of sin. I may not know all Your ways but I choose to follow the way You show me in my limited understanding. But merciful to me and show me the way to go, even at this moment.

February 2

Jesus, You remind me to have the simple faith of a child. It seems so simple, but I complicate it by not exercising trust in simple faith. You used a child to demonstrate Your point. My mind analyzes instead of asking. I see how You answer the prayers of others, but I overlook the simplicity of their belief in You. I ask that You help me believe as a child. Help me to know You will take care of me because of a love greater for me than You have for the birds of the air and the lilies of the field.

February 3

Jesus, I hear noise all around me. Some tell me how to live. Others tell me what I am missing. I want to bring You back to the center point of my life. You are all that matters and I try to make my life all about You. Other things will find their places once I make You first and foremost in my thinking and living. Help me to know You better so I can better understand myself and what my life is about.

February 4

Jesus, Your compassion was extended to those who followed You and those who died for You. Your name was on the lips of many whose last breath was finally taken away. I want Your name to be on my lips while I am living. "Let others see Jesus in me." I want that on my lips and also in my heart.

February 5

Jesus, You changed the lives of those who believed in and followed You while they lived. I want You to change my life more than it has ever been changed. Nothing can ever take Your place or make such a difference as You. I ask for Your peace to overwhelm my thoughts and outlook on life. I will be able to see a difference when I see life through Your eyes.

February 6

Jesus, You told us about an abundant life and You lived it. Even though I have You in my life, I sometimes don't experience living in abundance that You have for me. Open my eyes to see You, even in the things that seem to make little difference. Make my life more about You so I can experience more of life the way it was meant to be lived.

February 7

Jesus, I will never be able to fully understand Your death for so many. Your dying gave us a reason for living. I want my life to count for You. I pray that my life will make a difference because of the difference You made in me. I want to move more into a new level of understanding and living. You are all I need. You are all I want.

February 8

Jesus, I ask You to help me remove the excess baggage in life that really doesn't matter. I look for security in a life of uncertainty. Nothing is guaranteed except Your love for me. Oh, how I want to sense Your presence and feel Your love. Please don't withhold what You have for me. My lack of faith sometimes can be my biggest enemy. I don't need to be fighting against myself, but making my life all about You.

February 9

Jesus, I want to be confident that the work You began in me will be completed. Your will is not an order. It is something You desire for me. I want that more than anything else. Help me to see life from Your perspective and to live it the way You want me to live.

February 10

Jesus, You talked so much about faith while living. I seem to live life with little faith. You are all I need, but I keep looking elsewhere. I need to keep my eyes on You as this world takes its own course. I seem to be unhappy when I have every reason to be experiencing joy. You are my reason for living. Let me see the value of living and the value You see in me.

February 11

Jesus, You give me choices in life. One is to be happy. Happiness is being able to love myself as You love me. Others around me seem to know what life is about. I want my life to be all about You and to be happy while living. No one can bring joy and peace to my world like You. Thank You for offering it unconditionally.

February 12

Jesus, the one thing I ask for today is that it be a day of knowing You in an intimate way. I can't make it happen, but I can keep it from happening. I know it is a choice. I choose for this day to count for You so at the end of the day, I can count all the blessings You sent my way.

February 13

Jesus, help me to live in the moment for this moment. That may be the time You choose to reveal Yourself in a significant, but quiet way. I want to hear Your voice and see Your hand in the events that unfold before me. Let me look back on this day and say, "That was truly a God encounter." I don't want to miss anything or miss out on doing kingdom work You place before Me.

February 14

Jesus, You have me here on a mission. The mission field is where You have me at that particular time. I am unable to fulfill that mission if I am not there. Help me to see what I am to do wherever I am since that is my mission field for the moment.

February 15

Jesus, my journey seems to be so lonely at times. I can't say what I feel because of being misunderstood. Nobody knows but You. And that is enough. I don't understand Your ways, but let Your way and Your will be done. I don't want to experience anything outside of You. Help me to make my life all about You once again.

February 16

Jesus, my soul is weary and my body is tired. But I still have farther to go. I am not where I need to be, but I do try. Some days seem to be at a standstill when I look at how little progress has been made. Never let me turn away from You. Always be the Son in my eyes. Never let me go, even when I feel like I can no longer hang on.

February 17

Jesus, You have always been there for me. If you weren't, then I would not be where I am today. You ordered my steps, otherwise I would have wandered far from You. Keep me close to Your side. Help me draw unto You. I seek refuge from my enemies who want to convince me that You no longer control my life and I am outside of Your will.

February 18

Jesus, I know one day I will look back at this day and see how all things turned out for good in relation to Your kingdom work on earth. I want Your will to be done in me, even when others don't understand. I may not understand either, but the one thing I can do is trust You. That is the way I want to follow, trusting You all the way to the journey's end.

February 19

Jesus, death will soon come, but I want to live more for You until then. Once my life is over, so are my opportunities. I don't understand all about heaven or life here on earth. You ask for simple faith because You know my tendency is to complicate things. A child's trust settles it. Help me to settle things in my mind that cause me to be unsettled.

February 20

Jesus, I encouraged others when they were down and saw no way forward. They began to move on and later reconnected with You. I seem to be going nowhere at times, but I know I must move on. Help me to see progress, even if You choose not to reveal the place or the purpose of this next move.

February 21

Jesus, the night brings darkness to the soul. I don't know where to go. It even causes me to question where I am today. I know there must be more because of the abundant life that is available. The road has been weary and the journey long. I know I have less time than ever before. Show me how to make every day count and the direction I am to go. I don't want to miss You because I chose to make the wrong turns.

February 22

Jesus, You are my world and my life revolves around You. I so much want to know more about You and know You better. At times when I reach out, nothing seems to be there. I know faith is about the unseen. Help me see You when You are working all around and in me.

February 23

Jesus, You know me better than anyone. There are things I don't understand about myself or my circumstances. Sometime our circumstances shape us. But I want to be shaped by the Holy Spirit within me. That is my connection to You. That's how I want to be shaped and conformed into Your image.

February 24

Jesus, You are my strength. I sometimes feel as if I don't have the strength to live another day. It's not so much about my life, but about You living in me. Some see You in everything. Sometimes, I don't seem to see You working in any of my circumstances. I reach out and ask that You reveal Yourself so I will know You are still with me. I need an affirmation of You making Your strength my strength to face what the day holds.

February 25

Jesus, no one really cares for me like You do. Others gave up on me long ago, but You still linger. Your strength in me has helped me make it this far. I still have more road to travel. I need passion for the purpose of my life. Restore the joy of my salvation and a reason for living. Restore more to me than what the enemy has removed. Your supply is unlimited. Fill me and use me more than ever before.

February 26

Jesus, You will one day call me home. I will no longer occupy this body and this world. I will have a new body and a new life awaiting my arrival. Struggles will be over and tears will be wiped away. Help me make it to that day. I want to know You in a way so I can see the way You are making for me.

February 27

Jesus, when I chose to follow You, I didn't fully realize how You first chose me. A plan was already in place before I even knew You. Make the way clear as I try to follow You each day. I don't want to stop short of the finish line in life. I must make each day and each step of the way count for You. I have no more time to wander. Fill my days with an awe of Your work in my life. I want to seize the day and make it one that counts for the kingdom.

February 28

Jesus, help me not to listen to the chatter of others who say words that discourage me or try to downplay what You are doing in my life. I want nothing or no one to derail what You are doing in my life. I love You and my request is for You to give me assurance that I am doing the right thing and moving in the right direction.

March 1

Jesus, You know better than anyone what I go through or how I feel. My life and emotions seem to be in a roller coaster mode. I so much desire stability. You are the stabilizing factor, but my eyes stay on my surroundings rather than on You, my Savior. Save me from making just emotional decisions, but ones based on wisdom from above.

March 2

Jesus, You exchanged a regal robe for real flesh. You walked among us and did time on earth. I look forward to walking the streets of heaven and spending time for eternity in Your presence. Even though I don't see You, allow me to sense Your presence and Your Spirit.

March 3

Jesus, You grew in wisdom and size. You learned along the way. You knew all along Your mission. I sometimes feel as if I missed my mission, but I know as long as I seek, You will continue to unfold. Show me the way and what kingdom work You want me to do. I am Your servant in waiting.

March 4

Jesus, please come to my rescue. Deliver me from the traps of deception and the shackles of doubt. Open my eyes and allow me to see You at work. Open my ears to hear You speaking to my spirit. I know You are here because You live inside of me through the Holy Spirit. You chose me as an instrument. Play a melody on my heart's strings that is music to You.

March 5

Jesus, You know the path before me and where it is leading. You also knew before I began when it would end. You know how far along I am and what still lies ahead. I don't know how prepared I am and what remains. Somehow, let me get a better grasp on life. Hold me and never let me go.

March 6

Jesus, I have no one else who will listen. I really don't have someone who can talk to me because others have enough troubles of their own. I have so many questions and You are all knowing. I so much want to hear Your thoughts, possibly even see Your plans. I may not understand them, but I would like to know more.

March 7

Jesus, You are the Bread of Life. I hunger for a taste of what a life of abundance would be like. My soul is still not satisfied because I have not experienced a fullness of life the way You desire. I want more and I know You have more for me. Help me to close the gap and be drawn close to You.

March 8

Jesus, You helped hurting people. The Spirit that was in You is the same Spirit that is in me today. That Spirit gave You fullness and power. I ask for a filling and a fulfilling of Your Spirit. I need Your power to make it through life. But as I live, I want to live it to the fullest and make it worth living.

March 9

Jesus, I get weary of asking You so many questions about life and about myself. And I know You sometimes rather hear praises from my lips and a song from my heart. I want to make this day one that will be remembered as a result of a simple, but steadfast belief in You and Your promises.

March 10

Jesus, set my soul on fire with a passion to pursue You like I never experienced before. I want nothing to matter in life but You. I know once I become all about You, then a change will come about that I want experience. I know there must be more because You said there would be more for those who fully follow You. I present myself to You as a living sacrifice who wants to be wholly acceptable to You.

March 11

Jesus, You promised You would never leave me. You remain in Spirit and dwell within me. I sometimes feel so empty of Your presence and filled with other things not of You. I become filled with fear and anxiety. I become afraid. Help me to live in a way to know You and that You are always with me. I need to know of Your love for me and Your presence in me more than ever before.

March 12

Jesus, You wept. You know what it's like to be emotional. Inside of me becomes so fragile at times. I don't know if I can withstand any more pressure or distress. You were there when I was created. You know my inner most self. Help me to know how to live this life for You. I want it to count not only for something, but for Someone, and that is You.

March 13

Jesus, You are the Rock of my salvation. I need a solid foundation to withstand the storms of life that seem to be an everyday occurrence. I want to be a stabilizing factor to others who cry out for help. Give me the assurance that I can do all things through You, no matter what I go through.

March 14

Jesus, the world seems to be on a course of separation by going in the opposite direction from Your teaching. You told us and showed us. I want to be one that faithfully follows You to the end. I don't know where it may take me, but I know who is taking me. I give all of myself to You and to Your kingdom here on earth. Use me where I am. Place me where I need to be. Demonstrate Your love and power all the way through.

March 15

Jesus, my thoughts never escape You. You knew me before I was ever born. You know my thoughts before they are ever formed. Purge my thoughts that are not from You. Cleanse my heart when I fail to trust You or don't include You in everything. No one knows better than You. I want to know more about You and experience more of Your love than yesterday.

March 16

Jesus, You said You will return. Many try to determine the time and only live for the future. Help me to live for You today. I know You will be there tomorrow, but I need You now. Show me the way for today. I can only live in the present. Let me feel Your presence and make it a day worth living because You live in me.

March 17

Jesus, I can only imagine what my life would have been if I trusted You the way You put Your trust in the Father. He calls you "Son" and I am also one of His children. You asked Him to love us as much as He loved You. That shows how much You love me. I want to love You, even when I am feeling all alone. I know You are with me and You will see me through to the other side.

March 18

Jesus, You knew I would become weary and You instructed me to come to You for rest. I am weary and I certainly need to rest. I need it not only for my body, but also my mind. I become weary when my thoughts are worrisome. I search continuously for direction. I seek You for comfort. Give me the rest today that You said You can give. I ask for it now so I can have peace in my mind.

March 19

Jesus, hear my faintest cry. I have little left in me because of all the life that has been taken out of me. I hope every day that something will change. Only You know when that will happen. I just don't know if I can make it until then. Please show me or say something to let me know I can make it through this day and this dilemma.

March 20

Jesus, You asked help from Your Father when darkness was closing in and living on earth would soon come to an end. You were obedient and fulfilled Your purpose. I was created for a purpose also, one that is to be lived out on this earth. Show me the way while I am here and take me home to be with You when I no longer need to be here.

March 21

Jesus, You called others to follow You. I made an earlier choice to do so, knowing very little about where to go and what would be experienced on the way. Along with joy came sorrow. You were called a "man of sorrows," so You know how I feel at times. You overcame death. Help me to overcome my sorrow when I feel pain and not Your presence. Wipe away my tears and direct my steps when I can't seem to find my way to You.

March 22

Jesus, You changed the Apostle Paul's life in a way where he never doubted it was You. When I don't know the way, I sometimes doubt the earlier change I thought I experienced. Thank You for never having doubts about making Yourself known to me. Forgive me when I don't understand what is happening to me. Continue making a change in me and help me make it through.

March 23

Jesus, You called me by name before I ever called on Your name. You know me and my reason for being. Extend Your hand to me and show me the way. I know I can experience more if only I trust You more. The more I know You, life will become even more worth living. Thank You for being here with me along the way.

March 24

Jesus, to make a difference in life, I must allow You to make a difference in me. I live for You, but at times, I live for myself. I become self centered and selfish. It's not about me, but You living in me. Show me the way. Tell me what to do. Instruct me how to live this day. Let it count for You and make a difference so others can see it is You living in me.

March 25

Jesus, by You living in me means I can have peace. I know You, but I don't always experience peace and purpose. I know You will show me how to experience both. You died for me before I lived. Help me to live for You before I die.

March 26

Jesus, some day I will see You. Keep me close to You. I don't see You physically, but I want to know Your presence. I want to experience Your peace. I want to fulfill Your purpose for me. When others tell me what I am doing wrong, let me know what I am doing right. When I live for You, I know that is the reason for my being. Help me to be more and do more in Your name than ever before.

March 27

Jesus, keep me close to You. I will then know I am in Your sheltering arms and wrapped in Your love. Nothing can come my way or touch me without Your permission. You know what is best and know how to bring it into existence. You died for me so I can live for You. When I live for You, I know life will be more fulfilling.

March 28

Jesus, sometimes I don't think I see blessings from You. I go through days with my head down, never looking up, to see all the good things from above. What came from You is perfect and good. I want to look for You in all things more than ever before.

I will then see more of Your blessings that come my way. Help me to go on not just believing, but also seeing.

March 29

Jesus, You are my only hope. Some gave up on me earlier in life. Others still have doubts, yet don't give me the benefit of the doubt. I choose not to depend upon others for validation. You believe in me because of what You did for me. I so much want to know more about You and better understand what You have for me in the days ahead. I want life to be worth living and live more for You than ever before.

March 30

Jesus, I want an intimacy with You that goes deeper than anything I ever experienced before. I do thank You for this present relationship, but I know there must be more. I'm longing more for You and I no longer desire the things of this world. Some days I don't even like living in this world. I long for a life of peace with no pain. I can hope there is more because You are that Blessed Hope that can help me. I may not be able to see You, but oh, how I want to sense and know Your presence.

March 31

Jesus, I sometimes see myself as a failure more often than I want to admit. I know that is not the way You want me to live life or see it. But when I see nothing ahead, I wonder how I got here. You know where I am, even if I feel lost. Take me to the place where I can hear laughter again and feel the love of You through others. Lift my spirit and let Your Spirit move in me as You move me along in a life worth living once again.

April 1

Jesus, give me an infusion of hope that gives me a reason for living. Life can be seen as alive on the outside, and yet be dead on the inside. No life is sometimes seen in my eyes. Make Your fire burn inside me again. I want to acquire the fire that attracts others to You. The way is for You to be seen in me. Help me see how You are working in my life. Give me strength and direction to make the next move.

April 2

Jesus, You will always be who You are, regardless of my belief or unbelief. You don't leave me when I doubt and You won't leave me alone. I may only hear silence, but I know You are only a whisper away. Allow me to sense Your presence and hear Your voice. I need You this very hour. Let me hear You and feel Your touch to know all is well.

April 3

Jesus, You are all I need, but I continue to search for other things and other answers to my questions. No one knows better than You, yet I don't know why I keep hoping to hear something from others. Only You have my best interest and know what is best for me. Give me the patience to work out Your plan for my life and to see the purpose for my being. Only You can satisfy my soul. Only You can give me the peace as I fulfill Your purpose. Bring about calmness and clarity while You draw me nearer to Your side.

April 4

Jesus, no one can love me like You do, but I still look for love from others. I want acceptance from them, but they always have conditions. Thank You for Your unconditional love. You love me for who I am. Help me to love myself as You love me. I will never be perfect in the eyes of others. Thank You for Your perfect love for Me. You were beaten on my behalf, so help me not to beat myself up because of misspoken words or a misdirected step. You've never let me down and know You won't begin now.

April 5

Jesus, You calmed the storms on the troubled waters of the sea. Calm the storms in my troubled soul. The waves of worry pound relentlessly in my mind that causes instability in my thinking. Others seek peace in life. Help them see Your peace inside me that will cause others to seek You. I want my actions to be louder than my words. Live in me in a way so others will know there is more to living than mere existence. I want to live the way You want me to live. Show me the way, even today, in a way You have never revealed before.

April 6

Jesus, I read how You were brutalized beyond recognition. And yet some hardly recognize You living in me at times. This is not the way I want to live for You. I want others to see and hear You through me. I have no one to turn to but You. I want to be the witness that turns others to You and be able to see You the way You want to be seen through me.

April 7

Jesus, Your presence never diminishes even though I sometimes feel You are so far away. Thank You for dwelling on earth as one of us. Thank You for living in heaven so I can be with You forever more. Help me to enjoy the life You have for me here. Make it count for You a special way this very day.

April 8

Jesus, I long so much for the peace You said You would leave here on earth. I know it could help me live differently and see life from a different perspective. My prayer to You is for the days to become sweeter as they go by. I don't want to live with regret for any single day You left me here.

April 9

Jesus, I have people who say they sense Your presence in me. I know You live in me, but I don't exhibit Your power that is also available. Help me to speak with conviction and walk in confidence more than ever before. I want to feel Your presence, even when I feel alone. Help me to believe You want me to experience even more of Your peace and presence. I need You every hour, especially at this time.

April 10

Jesus, I will never understand what You went through on earth until I see You face to face. I will have no questions to ask You when I am able to see life from Your perspective. I need a glimpse of Your glory and a sense of Your love to help me make it through this silent time in my life. I don't hear You the way I did in the past. Silence stretches out over days where the only thing left is to hope. Allow what hope I have to lift me from the depths of doubt and discouragement. Put my feet on solid rock once again and stand firm against the enemy.

April 11

Jesus, You went through so much during the little time You spent doing ministry. You knew what You were facing, but continued moving forward. I hesitate with my steps in life because I am not sure if this is the Father's will for me. But I know this is where the trust factor separates so many of Your followers. Help me to move forward with the trust You had in Your Father so I can hear the words, "Well done."

April 12

Jesus, You know my heart's desire is to be a faithful servant. I falter at times, but I do not want to fail. I stumble and don't know how much longer these difficult circumstances will last. You do, so that is all that matters. I know some are seeing glimpses of Your glory. If You choose not to allow me that privilege, then somehow let me know You are with me.

April 13

Jesus, the way doesn't seem as clear as it did at other times. The Word says, "This is the way, walk in it." There are times when I don't know the way, or even Your voice. You traveled this way and faced every possible circumstance that could keep You from completing Your walk on earth. But You made it. You know where I am. You know my outlook. Give me renewed strength so I can mount up on wings of eagles and fulfill my mission on earth. I want to please You and it must be seen in my faith.

April 14

Jesus, You said You love me. This I do know. You know I love You, but it doesn't always show. I want to experience Your peace on earth. I long for that. I know there will always be confusion and chaos on earth, but it doesn't always have to be in my soul. Help me to experience the place that allows me to know today's bread will be provided. And yes, tomorrow's bread is not my worry. It will be there when I step into tomorrow.

April 15

Jesus, You showed us the way, but it is still difficult facing each day. I don't even know what the next hour holds, but I want to know there is no need to worry. I not only want to just know the way, but also to experience it. Make this day about You and less about my selfish desires and motives. I want to be drawn nearer to You and know it's not about me, but about You.

April 16

Jesus Your blood was shed for me. I know that's what the Word says, but don't fully understand why it had to be that way. One day when I see you, I will see the look on Your face and that will say it all. Help me to lay every encumbrance aside and run the remainder of this race well. I stumbled along the way and You never left me. You knew the reason for You dying, yet I don't know at times the reason I am living. I need hope. I need a glimpse of Your glory. Lead me the rest of the way home to You.

April 17

Jesus, this day is a gift from You for me to live. You died and were raised from the dead for me. Many saw a dead man walking when You rose from the grave. I want others to see a living Savior in me. Let them see my thoughts and actions guided by Your love. I don't want to just talk about the knowledge of knowing You, but a relationship I have with You. Feelings are part of the sensory system of our bodies. Let me feel Your presence all around me and know You are guiding me along life's pathway.

April 18

Jesus, You know me. You know my thoughts. You intercede for me in the heavens. Please intercede on my behalf while I am here. Keep me from danger and snares that may cause me to lose even more hope along the way. My faith becomes fragile at times. I want to live for You and be an example to others about the way to abundant living. I don't want to just talk about it, but to live it.

April 19

Jesus, You overcame this world while living among us. I am overcome at times with depression. I get overwhelmed by waves of discouragement. Rescue me from my present danger. Save me from the enemy's lies spoken to others about me. Give me strength and a willingness to never give up, not ever.

April 20

Jesus, I rejoice in You. I know I am not alone. The Word says You are with me every step of the way. Sometimes I don't know if I'm even on the right path. Keep Your hedge of protection around me when the enemy senses a vulnerability. I know he wants to destroy, but more importantly it is about Your saving grace. Thank You for the upcoming victory that is within reach.

April 21

Jesus, keep me safe. The journey in life is treacherous. It has slippery slopes and deep valleys. I made my share of mistakes and missteps. I don't want to go that way again. Teach me Your truths that protect me and prepare me for the day. Help me to keep swinging the sword and standing on Your words of absolute truth.

April 22

Jesus, You had a tender heart for people, but a tough resistance against those who came against You. I become weary of attacks from my enemies. I must stand firm and stand for Your truth. You told us and showed us how to live. I choose to follow You in this deeper walk. Take me deeper into those things from You. I want to know more of You every day in every way.

April 23

Jesus, You love me more than this mind will every comprehend. I don't even love myself on some days. Even on those days when I am hard to live with, You still love me. I want to live a life of selflessness where it is not about me. Let Your light shine through me that draws others to You. Make my life less about me and all about You.

April 24

Jesus, You said You would take care of our burdens as they are cast before You. The load is too great for me to bear. You didn't make me in a way to bear all that weight. You are here to help me along the way. I want to feel Your presence as You lift this from me. I turn to You this day and turn my cares over to You.

April 25

Jesus, Your enemies plotted along the way for evil against You. They meant to harm You, even to destroy You. I have no battle that is not already known to You. Show me each day, along the way, how You can turn what is plotted against me into Your good. I want my life to be worth the death You experienced on my behalf. I want to live more for You and have more of that abundant life You have for me.

April 26

Jesus, Your blood cleansed me from all sin, yet I continue in my sinful way of not putting my faith in You. I want to be faithful with my faith. No one knows me better than You. Help me to know Your ways so I can better serve You.

April 27

Jesus, You are all I need, but I still think about other needs in my life. I sense the need to know what life is all about. I question, but dare tell no one, what goes through my mind. If I falter, then I wonder what my life was all about in the first place. Before you remove me from earth, remove the doubts about You and Your work in my life.

April 28

Jesus, no one knows me better than You. You know how I ended up where I am, but more importantly You know why. My prayer today is to let all this work together for Your good and for the kingdom. Direct my heart and my steps to the place I belong. Let there be no more doubt in my mind that You were there all the time.

April 29

Jesus, You came to bind up the brokenhearted. Broken hearts leave behind a trail of tears. I cry alone at night. I cry inside during the day. No one hears because I choose not to let others know. Only You can bring healing. Thank You for being able to say, "I know," because You really know. Bring healing to my body, soul, and spirit. Let me laugh once again and know all is well.

April 30

Jesus, I don't know of any time I didn't need You. Yet so many of the times I failed to acknowledge Your willingness to help me. I lacked trust and didn't exercise my faith. I want to grow stronger in You by my faith becoming stronger. I want to be an overcomer and not allow the enemy to keep me down in my trust and faith in You.

May 1

Jesus, I know I can do all things through You who strengthens me. You are my help in time of need. Now is the time I need You to help me gain confidence that You are bringing about good things in my life in the form of blessings today. I want to soak in the mercy You poured out on me at Calvary.

May 2

Jesus, someday I will understand why the journey in life took me on this path that I now travel. I didn't choose this way, but this is where You have me for now. Tomorrow will be another day. I don't want this day to end until I learn what You are teaching and possess what You are presenting to me. I stand in need this very hour. Do not pass me by, but lead me to the Land of Promise.

May 3

Jesus, no one knows more about the toils and snares one faces in everyday living than You. As I lift my hands, I ask that You lift my spirits. I have so many reasons to be rejoicing over the things You have done, yet I feel lonely and isolated at times. Let me see Your goodness in a way that causes me to rejoice in the things You are doing and the way You are working in my life. Thank You, Jesus. I want to love You more than ever before.

May 4

Jesus, You said You will never leave me. Your presence is what I want to sense and to know Your love for me right where I am and for who I am. No one knows of my inner struggles the way You do. Keep me by Your side. Help me over to the other side. You are all I need and have no need to turn to anyone else. Strengthen me now as I try to make sense of this day.

May 5

Jesus, what a wonder You are. You can calm the most violent storm raging inside me. My enemies flee at Your command. I see the wonder of Your love for me. Help me this day to go where You want me to go and do Your kingdom work on earth. You chose me, so You have a purpose for Me. Help me to walk in boldness, knowing that I am taking back what the enemy stole from me.

May 6

Jesus, You suffered so I could be set free from the power of the enemy. Satan cannot doom me to a life apart from You. I want Your peace to engulf me and flood my mind with an overflow of Your love. No one knows the depth of my struggles. Give me the light of Your love and the plan You purposed here on earth for me. Let me walk in that light.

May 7

Jesus, You know more than just the thoughts in my mind. You know the motives behind my thoughts. I was washed in Your cleansing blood that flowed at Calvary. Move me from darkness to light so I can walk in truth. You set me free and that includes my mind. Help me to dwell on the thoughts of Your love for me. Awake, my soul, and rise up to know this love in a way I've never known before.

May 8

Jesus, You know how my thoughts turn to You every day. Life is hard and never easy for the downtrodden. You came to heal the brokenhearted. My heart feels shattered, but that is not the way You want me to live. I lift my hands and raise my spirit to a new level of experiencing You like no other time. Thank You for dying for me and giving me a reason to live.

May 9

Jesus, the more I know You, the more I can know about myself. I want to see life through Your eyes and live it abundantly that You make available each day. I want to be filled with Your joy and love. I know that I can overcome what the enemy tries to put in my way. Replace the enemy's traps in my mind with Your tender love and mercy.

May 10

Jesus, I struggle in life where there should be no struggles. My mind is in constant motion with thoughts about life, death, purpose, and direction. I will be with You in the end, but I need You as I make my way to that end. I want each moment to be lived for You and to be loved by You. I know Your love is there. Help me to live fully aware of Your presence, knowing You made a way, and I am walking in Your light.

May 11

Jesus, life is worth living when it is about You. You give me hope for tomorrow. Life lived out by You on earth demonstrated the way it is to be lived. Fill me with compassion and confidence. Show me the way when confusion fills the air and my mind. Make this day one that makes a difference, one that leads into a life of fullness.

May 12

Jesus, You are my Helper. I called upon You so many times in the past and You answered my prayers and pleadings. Thank

You for remaining and not abandoning me on this journey. Life is tough enough, but without You, it would be impossible to make it even one day.

May 13

Jesus, You know and see me. You also hear me when I call out Your name like a child in the dark. Your comfort gives me the assurance to keep moving forward. Your words light the path before me. Order my steps according to Your purpose. Help me to see You in all that I say and do. Guard my heart and lips. Let my words be a sweet, sweet sound to those all around.

May 14

Jesus, I know life is difficult as I pass this way. You have a place for me to be in the future days ahead. There is an assigned place and a specific task You equipped me to do. I gladly do it, knowing Your peace accompanies me as I fulfill Your planned purpose for me. I may have wandered, but thank You for not allowing me to stray from Your protection and sight. You were there when I needed You every hour, and You are there before I even cry out to You.

May 15

Jesus, You equipped me and called me, even before I was formed in my mother's womb. I was born at a specific place and time in history for such a time as this. Now that I am here, allow me to see how You created me to fulfill the task before me. I want to accomplish the mission I began when You formed me. It began before You placed me here. Help me to follow through and be faithful to the end.

May 16

Jesus, help me to have a pure heart that is pleasing in Your sight. Remove my iniquity by the cleansing that comes through Your blood. Your sacrifice allows me to stand before You as You sit at the right hand of Your Father. I desperately want to do His will and walk in righteousness. Show me how to better serve You and be at total peace. Give me the peace You left behind for me.

May 17

Jesus, I ask You to protect me from any possible harm the enemy has for me. He means harm and nothing good comes from him. Turn the possible evil into something that brings about good for the work of Your kingdom. I rejoice that You care so much for me and nothing will ever come my way without Your permission.

May 18

Jesus, You are the Potter and I am the clay. I am who I am because of the way I have been shaped during my lifetime. Continue to mold me and make me into Your image. I want others to see You before they see me. Let Your words be my words and my actions be pleasing to You.

May 19

Jesus, You are the One I know who has a better way for me than anyone else. I am unable to see beyond the present, while You know my future. I trust You to show me the way I should go that provides the abundant life You promised to those who live for You. Let me move toward You as You move within me. I trust You, not only with this day, but also the future days before me.

May 20

Jesus, hear my cry, see my tears, and heal this broken heart. I hurt so deeply inside at times and no one seems to care. Others don't ask, "How can I help you?" but "What can you do for me?" I've waited so long to see a change in my life. Give me the patience and understanding to make it until then. Help me to carry on until I see answers to my prayers.

May 21

Jesus, no one knows the prayers I prayed to You. They remain silent as I wait for answers. They may never come. But if they don't, then I have to believe there is a reason. I don't seem to hear from You as I did in the past. I don't know if You choose to remain silent or if there is a reason my prayers are blocked. Help me to search my heart as I seek Your face. Make known what I need to know and hide what does not yet need to be revealed.

May 22

Jesus, there was no more You could do for me, but there is so much more I can do in Your name. I focus too much on myself and not enough on the things You said are important. I sometimes don't see what You place in front of me because I am always looking at my circumstances. Help me see what I need to see and to help others along the way.

May 23

Jesus, loneliness is so much of my life. I often don't know who I really am and know even less about You. The more I know of You, the more I can better understand what You want me to do in this life. Keep me safe as I seek You. Help me not to waste what is from You and what life is about. I don't want my love to lessen for

You, regardless of the changes that come my way.

May 24

Jesus, the only way to the Father is through You. Thank You for providing this relationship and assurance. I know the way to please Him is through faith. That's where I need help from You. Others struggled with their faith while You lived among them. Help me with my faith while You reside in Me. I so much want to do what is right and know I am pleasing to You and the Father.

May 25

Jesus, one day I will meet You face to face. I don't know what look I will have on my face or thoughts that will be in my head. I do know that is the reason I am trying to make it through each day. I don't know the time or how prepared I will be. I don't even know if I will be better prepared tomorrow than I am at this moment. But when and where it takes place, I know it will be worth it all when I see You.

May 26

Jesus, You know my thoughts and my reason for being. I want to know more about You and how to better live for You. Many see You through others and I want to be one where they can see You in all that I say and do. Give me strength to be steadfast. Give me the wisdom to know what to do. Give me a better understanding of what You want to do through me, even at this moment.

May 27

Jesus, I so much want to sense the Spirit of God living in me. I need direction and a way of knowing that I am doing the right thing. Help me find You today in this confusing time and days of uncertainty. I do trust You because no one knows me better than You.

May 28

Jesus, I listen for Your voice and look for assurance to guide me when I have no sense of Your direction. My life is about You and I want You to show me what to do this day. Help me to trust You, regardless of what seems to be a world detached from You. I know You haven't abandoned me. Let me sense a smile on Your face to know You love me and I am doing what You want me to do for such a time as this.

May 29

Jesus, You questioned Your disciples when they had such little faith while in Your presence. My faith seems to drop more when the waves of doubt and uncertainty crash against my wall of faith. Help me to strengthen my faith in You and remove the doubts of uncertainty that erode the tenants of my faith. Strengthen what I once believed when I trusted You with childlike faith.

May 30

Jesus, fill my days with joy and laughter. I want to be one that encourages others to trust You for future direction and assurance. You are that Blessed Assurance. I know You are mine and I am Yours. Help me see this day as a more positive one, a day that I can say, "The Lord truly passed this way." I can't live on other peoples' faith, but I can be encouraged by their assurance of You living in them.

May 31

Jesus, I am very thankful to be a part of Your creation. Thank You for giving me life and making me alive today. I want to know You more than ever before. You kept me alive to this point and I know You have more for me to experience. Help me to make this time count for You. Be merciful to Me and help me be obedient to what You want to do in my life.

June 1

Jesus, I know there is a calling on my life. If I have a calling, that means I have been called. You set me apart to be a part of doing kingdom work here on earth. I know I am still here to complete the work You began in me. I don't want to miss out because I chose not to pursue You with all my heart. I do love You and want to serve You the rest of the days of my life.

June 2

Jesus, I have others who are depending upon me in this life. I can't stop or give up at this time. I must push forward to the end, knowing there is a reward You have for me. Please allow Your blessings to flood my soul. I don't want fear to overwhelm my faith. Keep me focused on the way You want me go and do the things You entrusted me to do.

June 3

Jesus, You talked about mustard seed faith. You knew I would be where I am today with only this small amount of faith left in me. I want to be all that You want me to be for You. Please make Yourself known to me and let me know all things are working out for the good and Your glory.

June 4

Jesus, will You allow me to have a peace that I never knew before? Faith is what I need when You seem to be silent. I sometimes wonder if I know Your voice anymore. You have never lost one of Your sheep. As the Good Shepherd, please rescue me from the lies and traps of the enemy. He wants to bring death, but I ask for You to bring life back to me.

June 5

Jesus, I don't know how many days I have left to live. It could be decades or just days. I could have many more miles to travel or just minutes left to live. Every moment is so important for me to know You. I see people so in love with You. I do love You, but each day I want to know a deeper love than the day before. I know You want the best for me. I must trust You more than ever before and make my life count for You.

June 6

Jesus, You had me on Your mind when You died for me. I have You on my mind, but it's in the form of questioning what my life has been about. I so much want to hear, "Well done" when I see You. I don't want to disappoint You here, so I won't be disappointed there. I love You, but I want to be more in love with You than ever before.

June 7

Jesus, I'm not even sure what today is about. You know where I will be tomorrow. When I close my eyes, I want to be able to say I did my very best and trusted You with all my heart. You know my heart and my thoughts. I want You to be able to smile when You see how I am trying to live for You. Be with me and let me really feel Your presence more than ever before.

June 8

Jesus, Your strength is what I need to continue this journey in life. I need Your love when I feel lonely. I so much want to experience hope since You are the Blessed Hope. I want to have a trust in You where I know all things are working out for the good and for the very best You have for me. Magnify Yourself in me so

I can see all that You are doing every day.

June 9

Jesus, You made strong comments about those who had great faith in You. You also said some strong things concerning ones who had less faith. Those closest to You seemed to be the ones You challenged. I know how close I sometimes come to giving up with no hope. That means I would lose so much of the "much more" You have for me. Help my unbelief and somehow bring about something that lets me know You are actively engaged in every detail of my life.

June 10

Jesus, place others around me who demonstrate an unfailing love and belief in You. I know others' faith won't get me to heaven, but it does raise my faith level here on earth. I want to be one where others see You as the One that my life is all about. I want to be desperate for You and not desperate in life. Be my Sustainer and Provider.

June 11

Jesus, increase my faith and enlarge my tent to hold all that You have for me. I don't want to miss anything or any way You want to bless me. I know there were blessings not released because I never released my faith at times when it was needed. Lift me from the pit that I find myself in more than I want to admit. I want to go from the pit to the palace like Joseph.

June 12

Jesus, You know my needs before I ever make them known

to You. I still speak things to You, Someone who does care and is willing to listen. I ask You to help me see this picture of life is bigger than me and yet somehow I fit into the plan You have for me. I don't want to think of myself as irrelevant, but one that You created with a purpose.

June 13

Jesus, I sometimes seem to have no real purpose. Creation looks to have a better order of existence than me. If the hairs on my head are numbered, then You know how many days are left in my life. I keep looking to the future, but today may be my future. If it ends today, I want to have lived it in a way that I have no regrets. Help me to look for You today and see You in a way You never revealed Yourself before to me.

June 14

Jesus, I want to have the confidence and comfort in knowing there are earthly rewards and heavenly blessings still yet to come before I die. I'm thankful for what You have done in my life, even though I sometimes don't think I've done much for You in this life. Place within me an expectancy that things will become better because I don't want to become bitter. Give me hope that the best is yet to come down from heaven to me on earth.

June 15

Jesus, help me to regain a confidence never experienced before. I become weary as my body becomes worn. I want to have a new lease and a new reason for living. At times life seems to be less meaningful than I originally anticipated. But life is not over and that means it's not over for me. Fill my heart with Your love and my life with a passion for You that I never fully experienced until now.

June 16

Jesus, the beauty of life surrounds me. I see color and formations. I sense the orderliness that was made out of initial chaos. The heavens and earth were spoken into existence. Man was made out dust. Speak life into my life. Show me the way for this very day. I know tomorrow will take care of itself because You care for me.

June 17

Jesus, comfort those around me who need a touch from You as I reach out to them. It's not about who I am to them, but who You are to me and also to them. I may be the only hope they see in a physical form. I look for You, while others may be looking at me to help them look for You. Help me to encourage others by sharing with them what You have meant to me and how they can experience Your tender loving care. Help me to continue to hope in You and point others to You, the Blessed Hope.

June 18

Jesus, You knew when I took my first breath in this life and also know the time for my last one. There is so much life I didn't fully live and missed opportunities to trust You. I have less time than yesterday. I want to be who You want me to be and not what I think I should be. Your plan is much greater than I could ever envision. I love You and want to experience all You have for me for this day. Tomorrow may never come. Today is all I have left.

June 19

Jesus, life is sometimes a mystery shrouded with a veil of uncertainty. I am puzzled and bewildered at the turns in life that come my way. Yet, because of Your grace and mercy, I can make it. I still have doubts about the remainder of the day. I know You will remain with me, regardless of what is in front of me. Give me calmness and a peace that can only come from You. Be my strength and guide me to an even higher ground of life and living for You.

June 20

Jesus, You made a way for me to see life from a bigger perspective. You didn't try to obtain the best things in life when you lived here, but presented us with the best way to live life. That way is when You live in me and through me. I am simply an earthen vessel, but with a heavenly light from above. Help me to show others the way to You since You are the only way to an abundant life on earth and eternal life in heaven.

June 21

Jesus, those who question my direction don't know what You say to me and where You direct me. They want reasons, but I have no clear explanation at times. I am simply going on what I sense You are saying to me. You sought Your Father's will and that is what I am trying to do. You were confident in your journey. Help me to trust You and be full of confidence. I may question You today, but in the end, I will have no questions because I will be in Your presence forever.

June 22

Jesus, I love You. I thank You for what is left in life that is planned for me. There are seasons in a year and seasons in life. Help me to gracefully exit the one I am leaving behind and to be grateful for the season I am now entering. There is a rhythm in life and a specific way I am to live each phase. When things seem to close in on me, help me to stay close to You.

June 23

I don't want to make a move that will detour me or place me in danger. Keep me safe and secure. I want to have a peace that overcomes anything that comes over me in life. Sustain me and take me into tomorrow with renewed hope and an even greater faith than I have today.

June 24

Jesus, You blessed me by how You lived among strangers and also those who knew You best. You were consistent and never ventured from the way set before You by Your Father. You asked Him to show us the way when You would no longer be here. I may be unclear at times which direction to go, but I know He has never deserted me. I want to increase my faith so I can increase my capacity to have a trust as never before. Let me sense Your guidance to overcome that which I seem to fear, even when You are near.

June 25

Jesus, You chose to live among us. You wanted to show us a better way. Life has no purpose or meaning outside of what You taught. You shared Your life which included a horrific death, but You broke the grip of death and the grave. You overcame the enemy's power over us. We are free to live freely and fully for You. I want to live a life full of purpose and one worth living. I feel so empty on some days, but that is the way I chose to live it. I want to have an ever increasing faith which takes me into realms of life that are fulfilling and full of the Spirit in me. Nothing will have a grip on me if I fully grasp what life is like with You in my life.

June 26

Jesus, I look around and see so many people with so many

needs. I see those who are begging for food. I see others who are brutal and break the will of people through their bondage. I want to be free from the things of the world that keep me down. Help my life be one that gives others hope and a desire to better understand themselves. Some have lost all hope that life will get better. Their conditions become worse and light becomes dimmer. Let me be a light to show them the way to You. Give me the words that bring hope and let them see You really care.

June 27

Jesus, when I go through a difficult time in my life, I want it to be something that can later be shared in a positive way. What the enemy meant for evil, I know You can turn into good. I love You and know all things, even what I am facing now, will be for the good of Your kingdom and me. I don't know how I made it through some of the difficulties I earlier encountered. You saw me through and turned it into a situation where some of the most difficult times were overcome. I made it through then, and with Your help, I will make it again.

June 28

Jesus, so many times I call upon You only when there is a need. I want to make my daily communion with You one of honored praise and worship. I want my spirit to be in tune to Your every word and gentle nudge. Speak to me this moment as I say thank You for who You are and all that You are to me in life.

June 29

Jesus, there are so many distractions in life that remove my focus from You. Changed lives have resulted for many generations because of You. I not only want my life to change more dramatically for You, but also to help others make a change toward

You. Death was something You faced, but it didn't cause You to be distracted from Your mission. I want my life to be more about You and less about distractions.

June 30

Jesus, life is difficult, even when I know You. I don't see how others live outside of You. Some may choose not to pursue You because of my choices in life. Help me be the one that someone today will ask me why my life is different and not filled with distractions. They will see it as I allow You to make a difference in me. Thank You for being in me and living through me.

July 1

Jesus, when others talk about You, I want You to speak through Me. You can make life worth living for those who constantly struggle. You can bring peace and life with meaning and purpose. Uncertainty looms over the horizon for this world, but it becomes even more paralyzing when seen from one's personal horizon. Help me today to steady my life's ship and see how You will be with me through the upcoming storm. Nothing can touch or harm me outside of Your permission.

July 2

Jesus, I have seen Your healing power work in the lives of others. I know You did the same thing for me. Bring about healing to me where I need a touch from You. At times there seems to be physical, emotional, and mental damage. Even a spiritual dryness overcomes me. Thank You for bringing about the healing needed now to live the remaining days of my life serving You.

July 3

Jesus, Your friendship is what I desire today. I feel lonely, even in a crowd where people's daily activities occupy their minds. I think about You regularly and so much want to know You more than ever before. Draw me closer to You. I want to know Your presence in a way where no doubts arise and no anxiousness is felt. Gently make Yourself real to me and help me live with the assurance that my steps are now being ordered by You.

July 4

Jesus, the love of You for me is what gives me the reason to want to live another day. There seems to be an absence of Your love, even though I know it has not diminished since the day You died for me at Calvary. The love of You for me lets me know there is a reason for continuing this journey in life. Present Yourself in such a way that I can say, "Truly the Master passed my way today. I felt His presence and sensed His love."

July 5

Jesus, You know how much longer I have to live and the kind of life I will live. Help me live every moment with You in mind. Every day is precious because I am not guaranteed tomorrow. Keep me aware of living the life and in the light provided by You. I want this day to count for You and to do something special for You because of all You've done for me.

July 6

Jesus, You have always been there for me. You know what I go through. You know the moment my eyes shift away from You and when my troubles become a burden. My heart becomes heavy and my eyes turn to sadness. Help me to raise my eyes and see You take my hand to lead me the way I am to go. You are the main reason I want to live today, a day that I hopefully will know You really did pass my way.

July 7

Jesus, I made it to this place in life because of the way You made me. So much around me causes me to become distracted. Everything I experience in life can be a lesson. I want to learn each one so I don't have to pass this way again. Lessons are for living. I humbly ask that I can laugh today and make a joyful sound that can be heard by others and You.

July 8

Jesus, my heart longs for a relationship with You where peace abounds. I want to go to sleep at night, knowing I am resting in Your arms. I also want to awaken, realizing the day is one where You will direct my steps. Help me to know You more so I can know more what my life is to be about and how I can best serve You.

July 9

Jesus, I know I have been forgiven, but I want to experience it more. The enemy has a way of unloading guilt on me while I am trying to sense You during those times. I feel isolated when sin isolates my mind from Your compassionate forgiveness. I want to experience You even more when the enemy tries to convince me how You love me less because of my wrongdoing. I am forgiven because no sin is greater than Your spilled blood's ability to cover it.

July 10

Jesus, touch me again in order for me to know Your presence and Your power. I am an overcomer who has yet to experience all of You in a way that any obstacle in my life can be overcome. Peace is what I desire. Forgiveness is what I want to sense. You died with my sins on your mind. I want to live with Your forgiveness on my mind. You are here all the time for me. Use me where You have me at this moment. Help me to complete this task so I can move on to a higher plane of living for You.

July 11

Jesus, help me to make today more about You and less about me. I want to glorify Your name and sing praises to You. Help

me be at peace with You and believe that today I can do all things
through You because of who You are and whose I am.

July 12

Jesus, I feel like a stranger in a strange land while on this
journey. I feel isolated and uncertain. I'm not sure what to do or
where to go at times. Be near to me. Let me know that You know
what You are doing and where You are taking me.

July 13

Jesus, the uncertainty of life causes me to be uncertain about
You. I know what I am experiencing, and I so much want to experience You. I want to know You more and know more about my
calling and Your direction for me in life. Guide me safely through
the storms and gently show me the way to go. Open my heart to
receive more of Your blessings set aside for this day.

July 14

Jesus, You know when my heart is troubled and also when I
trust You. I want to have so much faith that one day You can say,
"Well done." I try to do my best and follow Your voice. Help me
to hear Your words very clearly and know You are with me. I do
feel lonely when I am uncertain of Your nearness. Draw me close
to You as I draw closer to the place prepared for me in heaven.

July 15

Jesus, I know faith is the key to abundant living. I so much
want an abundance of faith that will see me through every storm
and every dry land on this journey. Help me to know You are be-
side me, seeing my steps and hearing my pleas. I can't give up now

because I've come too far to turn around. I must go on.

July 16

Jesus, You have me on Your mind, even when my mind is on everything but You. I look for peace on the outside, but it is inside of me because there is where You dwell. The Father's house has many rooms. I am one of those rooms where You reside.

July 17

Jesus, I try to live for You each day, even on the days that seem more difficult than others. Your love for me never changes, even on those days I became unlovely. You know my heart and what I really want to be for You. Take me and make me an instrument of praise and worship to You.

July 18

Jesus, I come to You on bended knee and bowed head. Life has crushed me like the petal of a flower during a rainstorm. I may be drenched, but not drowned. I am overwhelmed, but not overtaken. Give me strength for one more day. Help me see what You see and do what You want me to do. I ask this and do all in Your holy name.

July 19

Jesus, I want to experience days where I can bask in Your love. I wish I could see You so You can wrap Your arms around me and draw me closer to Your side. Press into my spirit with Your Holy Spirit so I can know in a tender and loving way You are with me this very moment. Help me not be overcome with fear, but have a spirit of faith that trusts You in all my ways.

July 20

Jesus, You speak to others through other people. I want to be able to speak confidence and love to the hearts of those who are struggling around me. They look for some sign about how to face their dilemmas. I look for hope and encouragement from You. Help me pass that on to those who desperately want to know if anyone truly loves them.

July 21

Jesus, You never lied. You spoke truth and said You were the Truth. I must then believe the promises You spoke. I read them, but that is not the same as believing them. Help my unbelief and to know those promises are for me. Thank You for telling the truth.

July 22

Jesus, I become lost at times along the way. Where I thought I was going eventually changed. Anticipation turned into anxiety. Determination dropped to the level of doubt. Mistakes sometime led to misfortune. But through it all, I am still traveling this journey. Make my path straighter so I can better see where I am being led. Listen to my cry as it pierces the dark nights of loneliness. Draw me closer to You, dear Lord, close to You.

July 23

Jesus, Your words in are the Word and I must make them part of my belief system. I am here today only because of how You provided and protected me along the way. I would not be here if You had not brought me here. I don't know where I would have been. Let me know Your presence and Your purpose. I want to be and do all that You have for me the remaining days here on earth.

July 24

Jesus, darkness seems all around me, even when there is daylight. You order my steps and I try each day to live accordingly. You have blessings that will be released when I exercise my faith. To have more blessings, You said I only need faith the size of a mustard seed. I take that amount of faith and lift it up to You today. It's small and simple, but that seems to be all I have. Please let me see a miracle and an acknowledgment from You that I am still loved and accepted by You.

July 25

Jesus, I don't understand all what You are now doing and how You will return. I want the Holy Spirit to be as much a part of my life as You when I accepted You as my Lord and Savior. I need comfort, but I also need direction. I want to be full of compassion, but also full of confidence. Make me a strong warrior that You trust and know I will do what is commanded.

July 26

Jesus, allow the beauty of my relationship to You be experienced by me and seen by others. When I pass someone's way, let that person know it was an encounter with You. Let there be peace and hope that is desperately needed by so many today. Let them see me as one fully trusting in You. Hold me close to You, as close as You hold my future.

July 27

Jesus, no one cares for me like You. No one has personally died for me and demonstrated how life is to be lived. I don't want to disappoint You by the life I live. I can't relive the past, but I can realign myself to live according to Your teaching. I want to be all about You and to do so, I must be more like You.

July 28

Jesus, You said You are the Way. That was a bold statement made by You and one I want to experience in my daily living. I seek to know Your way each day I live. Each moment is precious and cannot be relived ever again. I want this day to count for You. If it does, then I know I won't be able to count all the blessings that come my way. Help me to know You better so the way will become more clear.

July 29

Jesus, place Your hand of mercy on me. Cover me with Your protection. Direct me to the land of milk and honey and let me taste the sweetness of victory. I want to know the feeling of knowing that I confused the forces of darkness and I now walk in mercy and goodness. They are what I want to be wrapped around me. You know what is best for me. Your best is always the best.

July 30

Jesus, You know the length of my days. You know what I missed and what I have yet to experience. Mountaintops are more appreciated after time in the valleys of life. Please make today a mountaintop experience so it will help me know why these struggles in life are worthwhile.

July 31

Jesus, I may not see Your return here on earth, but I will see You in heaven. Life has been difficult, especially when experiencing darkness and times of emptiness. Give me joy and laughter and see this life on earth is meant to have full meaning also. Remove the blinders of doubt, the yoke of a heavy heart, and the feeling of confusion and uncertainty. Be my strength today because I have very little in me.

August 1

Jesus, You love me. I know that, but I also want to feel it. I want to feel love deep down in my soul. I am Your child. Draw me close to Your side and help me know that no weapon formed against me can ever penetrate Your shield of protection. Deflect the fiery darts of deeds and words against my mind and away from the path I travel today.

August 2

Jesus, I want this day to be one when I will look back and say, "Thank You. Thank You." I have so many reasons to be thankful, but I pray You will let this day be a special one. Lift my head and lift my spirit, something I feel like I can't do alone. I thank You in advance and praise Your wonderful name. Thank You, Jesus.

August 3

Jesus, You knew when Your life on earth would end. You made sure You accomplished the Father's will prior to that time. Help me to be able to say, "It is finished" when my time ends. I want to fulfill Your plans and not just be a life what I wanted it to be.

August 4

Jesus, You know my needs. But more importantly, You know when and how they are to be met. Sometimes I wonder if my current needs will ever end because of the amount of time they have been in my life. Send a shower of blessings that will satisfy this parched soul which longs for all the good things You have for me.

August 5

Jesus, I spent many years telling others how You will take care of them. You've taken care of me and that is something I will never deny. But I ask that I can see You as a "much more" God the remaining time I have left. I always wanted a simple life. That's not a life without, but one where I rest in the assurance that I simply trust You and have no worries about tomorrow.

August 6

Jesus, I lived for so many years with thoughts about how I perceive You. The longer my life span continues, the less those perceptions have become. You know what it's like to live a life on earth with confidence and commitment. Help me to have more of those in the time I have left. I don't want to end with regret, but an assurance from You that all will end well.

August 7

Jesus, if someone was able to see what is on the inside of me, a different me would be seen. I try to keep the faith, but so many times I have little left in me. You trusted me with a specific plan and the gifts to accomplish it. I want to increase my quality of life by not burying what You provided that is to be multiplied. Help me be a good steward, beginning even now, and look for opportunities to live life more fully committed and confident.

August 8

Jesus, I look for Your return and with a belief that life will be perfect with You. Help me to have the faith and confidence while I wait for You. You died for me. I try to live for You. I want my faith to please You so much that You want to hasten Your return. I do love You and please help me make it to the other side.

August 9

Jesus, touch me again. I've known Your presence and knew it could be no one but You. I sometimes don't sense the presence of Your presence. I know I'm not to go merely on feelings. Somehow let me know all is well, even when things don't seem to be going well.

August 10

Jesus, You loved me in such a way that cannot ever be denied. So many times I denied Your power to work in my life because doubts overcame my faith. It was a choice given to me, but given my situation, I made some wrong choices. I want to make right what I made wrong because of wrong choices. Let Your forgiveness flood my thoughts so I can truly sense Your presence in my life.

August 11

Jesus, Your were present when creation was made. Make me an instrument to receive and be a channel to give to others. Help me to look at my blessings and share the goodness with others. Let me live full of Your love and share Your love. I know I will receive more when I am willing to give more.

August 12

Jesus, let me live long enough to live the life You meant for me to live. I sometimes wonder if the struggles and dark valleys are worth what little time I may have. Keep me close to Your side until I make it to the other side. In the meantime, share with me what You want me to do for You. Let me know this will be worth it all.

August 13

Jesus, sometimes I want to see too far in the future or dwell too long in the past. Life is about the present and that is where I want meet You. I wait in silence for Your words to speak to my spirit. I listen with the hope of learning more about who I am and what I am to do at this time in my life. Let me enter into Your presence for this present moment. I want to feel Your love wrapped all around me.

August 14

Jesus, You said to put my trust in You. I have no one that I can trust like You, but it is still hard to do. It's the invisible world that keeps me from fully putting what faith I have left in You. My faith seems to have been stripped down to a bare thread. That's all I have, but that is also all that You need. Use this single strand of faith for the bountiful blessings You have for me.

August 15

Jesus, for all the days I have not trusted You for my future, please restore those days the locusts have eaten. I want to bear the fruit from the seed of life You planted in me. Restore all that was lost. Repair the walls that were broken down. Let me see more sunrises so I can have more time to see all the good You have placed before me.

August 16

Jesus, You faced trials and darkness in life, and You knew You would be with the Father after Your time on earth was over. I know I will be with the heavenly Father also, but I still struggle with the daily battles. Help me today, knowing that tomorrow will have enough troubles of its own. I need You because of the needs I face today. Be with me and help me know You are here with me.

August 17

Jesus, a thousand years will only seem like a day with You in heaven. But on earth, a day sometimes seems like a thousand years. A minute turns into an hour with the same questions. You want more of me, and I certainly need to sense more of You. At the end of the day, I want to say with real meaning that You passed my way and I made the day count for the kingdom.

August 18

Jesus, what comprises the day is never known until that day is lived. I may be unable to know what Your plan was for me until that plan was lived. I won't know until I pursue what You have before me. It can only be the best and I don't want to leave life without it.

August 19

Jesus, You spoke truth and You told us how to live when You dwelt among us. Your words in the Word are still true today. The enemy tries to focus on regrets and bad planning on my part. You are the reason I continue and believe tomorrow will bring a better day. I want to feel joy in my heart and hear Your thoughts in my mind again.

August 20

Jesus, as others look to me, help me to look to You. Some who don't know how to hear from You may look to me to see what I may be hearing. Let Your voice be clearly heard and Your words ring in my ear. Life is complicated and too fragile to push ahead with no direction and no input from You. Make my spirit attentive to the things the Holy Spirit is speaking to me.

August 21

Jesus, some days I make it about me. I approach them as though Your decisions are based upon my personal needs. It's not about me. It's about You. You died so I could live. I want to live for You before I die. You know the amount of time left for me to live. Let this day be the first day for more of life than ever before. I've lost much time. Help me redeem what time is left and let it be lived for You.

August 22

Jesus, one day You will call my name. It won't be an option for me. You know the time and where I will be. Will I rejoice or sense regret? I know it will be worth what I went through, but will be nothing compared to what You went through. Thank You for enduring until the end. If I knew what awaits me, I know I would focus less on the present and more what is beyond that dot on the line of life when my life ends on earth. Take me home as You take me into eternity.

August 23

Jesus, there was a specific purpose, a mission to accomplish, while you lived here. It was accomplished and now You are back home again. I left home many years ago and thought I would be enjoying the fruits of my labor. I have less now than I possessed earlier in my life. I don't know where and how this will end for me, but You do. I can only trust that my mission will be completed on earth before I enter heaven.

August 24

Jesus, I love You. You did so much for me and I know You desire for me to know You in a more intimate way. Show me how to better sense Your presence. Let me move into another realm of knowledge and relationship with You. I don't know the next move. If I can't move toward You, please draw Your presence near to me.

August 25

Jesus, I see the beauty of creation all around me. This did not come about by mere chance or accident. You didn't let me come about without purpose. There is a reason the earth has an existence. The same is for me. I was made for a reason. Let me see the way You see me. I want to trust You as much as You trusted me with this plan for my life.

August 26

Jesus, every day I live is a special day. It comes from You and is given to me to spend it freely. I want to be wise in my choices and protective of my words. I want to have a pure heart and pure motives. Shine through me and spread Your love to those who know it could only come from You.

August 27

Jesus, You place people in my path that can only come about because of Your love for me. I know those times are not merely incidental or by accident. It was truly You who passed my way. Let me see You when You choose to reveal Yourself through another person or situation. I need to know. I need to see. Help me to continue and believe.

August 28

Jesus, life has been described as a vapor. That is not a lot of longevity on this earth. I missed out on many days. I want each one to count more and more as I pass through them. Give me hope so I can live in a way that gives hope to others for that day.

August 29

Jesus, there are some who want You to come quickly, and others who want more time on earth. I want to be here long enough to be who You created me to be. There has to be more to life than this because You said life could be lived abundantly. That means much more. Let me know You more so I can live a life much more pleasing to You than ever before.

August 30

Jesus, You blessed many during Your time of ministry on earth. You certainly ministered to me during my time here also. Let me sense Your presence and see You working through me even more. Things just don't happen by coincidence, but because You cause all things to work together for the good. Thank You for Your goodness.

August 31

Jesus, my prayers usually begin with "Bless me." I choose today to say "Blessed be Your holy name." The walk of holiness is a walk I desire for my life. I want to be like You so others can fully see me as one who is loved by You and is a life they can experience also with You. I don't want anyone to steal my joy, but rather be full of joy and hope. I rejoice now in Your presence.

September 1

Jesus, You never said it would be easy, but never did I know it would be this hard. I hoped for a life of cheer, but at times, it has been more of chaos. Yet that may be where I hear You the clearest and know You the deepest. Give me the peace that only comes from You. Help me to have hope, especially during those times when hope seems to have escaped me.

September 2

Jesus, I look for stability this day to know I am on solid ground and making my way toward You. Life is in constant motion and I must continue. I want to move closer to Your will for me so I can say, "This is what He was doing all this time." You know my heart and now I respond to the Holy Spirit. Help me give more of my hopes and dreams over to You so they can become what You want for me.

September 3

Jesus, You experienced a constant barrage of criticism from Your enemies and continuous questions from Your followers. You knew Your identity and Your mission in life. Give me a better understanding about myself and not allow things that will bring into question who I am in You. You know the way. Show me. You know the truth. Share it. You know where I am to be at this time in my life. Send me. Let this life be all about You.

September 4

Jesus, I no longer choose the way others want me to go or do what they expect of me. You know best and what is best for me. That is what I pursue and what I desire. You know every move I make and every thought I think. I choose to make all these things all about You because no one cares for me like You.

September 5

Jesus, I've read about You most of my life. I've studied the Word and tried to share my witness. I want my relationship to be as fresh as the morning dew, yet strong enough to last for a lifetime. I want to feel Your love and sense Your mercy. I don't always hear when I think I really need to hear. I don't want to move in the wrong direction or miss the direction You place before me. Never let me get out of Your sight. Never let my ears become deaf to Your voice. Help me to trust You for everything and in every way.

September 6

Jesus, the way seems uphill. I sometimes don't know how much longer I can continue. I wake up, hoping the way will become clearer. I do know the journey is getting shorter. I want each day to count for You, knowing it may be my last. I surrender all of myself to You and shape me into the vessel You desire me to be. Mold me and make me, even if it means breaking me. Help me to never give up.

September 7

Jesus, the path I travel seems to have few travelers. I can't ask others where it is leading since we all have personal destinies. I cannot tell others specifically when life will end. But I can tell them where I've been. I was encouraged along the way, sometimes very little and at times by only a few. Help me to trust You and have a testimony about how You never gave up on me.

September 8

Jesus, I know others may sometime see me the way I see my-self. They don't see the confidence that once came easier than it does now. My words don't seem to be as assuring. I know You've never left me. Help me to live fully alive in Your presence. Let Your presence go with me and never diminish or go away. You never change. I want to be so confident in life so I can say with total assurance that You will never let me down or let go of me. Thank You for that kind of daily walk available to me.

September 9

Jesus, I made it this far, even though I didn't know the path of life would take me in this direction. I am here and You are still here with me. I want Your peace to rule in every corner of my being. I want to maintain the direction You keep moving me. Help me not to stand still when You are directing me. Also, give me clarity when I am to be still. I've lost time along the way, but I know I will arrive in Your time.

September 10

Jesus, Your love covers my grief. Your mercy allows my sins to be forgiven. Your tenderness soothes the aching soul. You have so much to share and want to give me. I don't feel I have given You what You deserve from me. I want so much of You and yet You ask so little from me. I want to be all about You because there is nothing more important in my life than You.

September 11

Jesus, the mention of Your name gives me hope. The love You have for me is hard to grasp. My hope lies in You because I try to make life all about You. Help me to see You are in more control of my life than I realize. I ask that every step be ordained by You. I don't want to go anywhere or do anything that will cause me to miss the way or miss You. Keep me close to Your side and under Your protection.

September 12

Jesus, I need a touch from You. I so much want to know my life is not being lived randomly, but was ordained by You before my life ever began. I want to make each day count for You. It is my prayer that others will see You in me. I ask for an overpowering sense of Your presence. Hold me close and somehow speak to me. Let me know that everything will be okay and I am pleasing You this very moment.

September 13

Jesus, it is said that joy comes in the morning. And morning comes when there is light. There have been many dark days, much of it because of my own doing or thinking. I want to have Your mind, one that fully entrusts my life to the heavenly Father. Trust is what I have given You for my life and my future. Speak to my heart today so I can know I am loved and You are bringing about the blessings You have for me. I want to be a blessing to You and I will know I am blessed.

September 14

Jesus, I get tired, but I can't give up. I believed in You when I was young and had simple faith. As I become older, my faith seems to waver when it should be getting stronger. I may end this life with less than I earlier possessed, but I want to have more faith that ever before. I don't know how to get it back, but can only trust that You will not give up on me. Help me hold on to the faith I do have. I want to know You will be waiting for me with open arms and a love that can only come from You.

September 15

Jesus, others look at me and wonder if I am who I was meant to be. At the moment, only You can answer that question. I try to believe I am being directed by You. I am not sure some of the time, but I keep moving forward. You blessed me many ways along the way, so I choose to believe I've walked in Your ways. Thank You for Your grace when I didn't know any better. I really tried and I believe I will be honored on that day.

September 16

Jesus, I pass many people in life. I wonder what they see when they see me. I want them to see You and sense Your peace. Calm my spirit within me. Give me wisdom so my words will provide the needed direction and answers others may be seeking at this time on their journey. Help them see and hear You through me.

September 17

Jesus, I can't do anything about the past. I don't know anything about the future because it has not yet been revealed. The only time I am given is the present. This present moment will soon pass and it will be another moment that passed by me. I want to make the best of what is before me before it moves behind me. Help me to cherish what You are bringing about this moment. I love You and long to see You and hear You say, "Well done."

September 18

Jesus, You gave me instructions on how to live. You even

demonstrated it here on earth. But life has become so complicated. There are so many issues to deal with and more decisions to be made. I need direction and wisdom. Help me not to move too quickly and yet not wait too long. It's not a guessing game, but a life of trust. I want to trust You more than ever before and I need direction as never before. Show me and help me to walk accordingly.

September 19

Jesus, my mind has a way of wandering away from my basic beliefs. I have more questions and seem to have fewer answers. I will never know some things until life is over. That is when life will be in Your presence and I will have no more questions. I want to have the faith of a small child once again. I want maturity, yet meekness also. Give me strength and a will to be submissive. Help me to be the person You created me to be.

September 20

Jesus, I become weary along the way. I also become fearful. I have a fear of not being or doing what You set before me. I chose what I thought You wanted me to do. I made the best decisions I could at the time. I tried to be different and not waste my life away. Some may see it as a waste, but they don't know my desire to really please You. I trusted You as my Savior and I am still trying to follow You. Help me not to give up now.

September 21

Jesus, You have been my whole world. I kept You foremost in my mind and made decisions I thought were best in Your name. I don't know what else to do or anywhere else to go. I am where I am because this is where my journey has taken me. Meet me where I am and lead me the rest of the way home.

September 22

Jesus, I know You were raised from a tomb meant to contain You. At times, I sense as if I am in a darkened tomb, never to rise again to the joy of living. The darkness of depression and discouragement keep me from seeing how Your purpose for me is being fulfilled. Help me rise above what is holding me down. Let victory soon triumph over the tomb as it did for You.

September 23

Jesus, You sit at Your Father's right hand, seeing me as one You came to earth to bring into Your kingdom. Thank You for caring that much for me and loving me so much that You could never love me more than You do now. I seem to love You less when I feel Your presence less. I know my relationship is not just about emotions, but a faith that endures for the One who loves me forever.

September 24

Jesus, lives were changed forever when You appeared as one of us. Now that I am part of You, I want my life to never be the same again. Remove the doubt and the uncertainty about You. I believe enough to die for You because You loved me enough to believe in me. I don't want to bring disappointment, but to display an unfailing love for You.

September 25

Jesus, You are the only way, yet I hear others claim to know other ways to God. You were with Him, later revealed Yourself here and then returned to heaven. I trust no one how to get me home but You. I know You won't give up on me, so help me believe until the end. Give me grace for this moment.

September 26

Jesus, You allowed the enemy to put an end to Your life. The same enemy wants to do the same thing to me. Victory was experienced by You in the end. I want to leave this life victoriously when it comes to an end also. I know death is certain, but it will certainly not be the end for me. I look for the day to see You in all Your glory and be in Your presence forever.

September 27

Jesus, Your compassion is hard to comprehend. Your love for those who crucified You never wavered. I waver. I wonder, sometimes to the point of feeling lost and lonely. I know You are with me. There is no reason to feel apart from You since I became part of You and Your kingdom. You are my reason for living. I want to be fully alive and fully consumed. I want to be all about You and nothing else. You matter most.

September 28

Jesus, You never offer me broken promises, but only those that can be fulfilled. Sometimes the best I can offer You is broken praise. I try to praise You when I am going through brokenness. My heart may not be in it when it has been ripped out of me. Take my broken praise as the mustard seed. Please use it to honor You, even when You are humbling me.

September 29

Jesus, I have staked my life and my future on You. It seems so foolish to many, even those who say they trust You also. It's easy for them to say that when blessings continue to engulf them with things they want in life. It's hard for me to trust when those things I believed You for in life have never fully become part of my life. It may not be too late to receive those specific things that were in my prayers most of my life. Whatever the outcome, I can honestly say I tried to be and do what I believed was from You. Please let see me Your love, even when I see nothing else being brought forth.

September 30

Jesus, You are the Bread of Life. I need life brought back into everyday living. You took the bread and broke it before thousands. I feel like I have been broken before multitudes of others. But miracles came as a result of the breaking process. Help me to been seen by others as one You blessed and was worth whatever breaking process You allowed in life.

October 1

Jesus, the kindness of Your words and the healing from Your touch forever changed many people. You brought healing to me and Your words comforted my troubled soul. Speak to me as I speak to my circumstances. Help me as I live in a world of hurt, inside and out. May my life touch others when they see You as the One who can forever change them here and for eternity.

October 2

Jesus, the grace You brought down to me will also one day take me up to You. Your grace is sufficient. Let it be there when I encounter difficulties. Allow it to linger as I regain my strength and become reoriented while on this journey. You have never failed and know You are not about to begin now. Thank You, blessed One.

October 3

Jesus, I mention Your name with my lips and speak it into my thoughts. You are the nearest and the One who loves me the dearest. Thank You for all You have done and I thank You in advance as I am enabled with kingdom living. Thank You for Your never failing love and for Your mercy that endures forever.

October 4

Jesus, You brought light into darkness. You gave me living water when I thirsted after You. I want all of me to be about all of You. Never forsake me nor leave Me. Help me not to abandon the hope and dreams placed within me when You came into me. I live for what You promised. I know it will happen at the right time. Let my heart be right for You and for all that You want to do.

October 5

Jesus, You saw creation come into existence and You were there when I became part of the creation process. I was placed at this time in history for a purpose that is to be fulfilled in this life-time. You know the remaining time and You know what remains to be done. Bring about today what needs to be in place before I face tomorrow. My steps are ordered with a certain order. Help me not to falter, but to be faithful, even when my steps seem to be moving me in the wrong direction.

October 6

Jesus, Your name is above all names. That is why I call upon Your name. You know me. You died for me. You intercede for me when I don't know what to say or where to go. I call upon You to move me from discouragement to a life with direction. You made no one like me and no one can live my life for me. Bring joy and laughter. Put a smile on my face and sunshine in my life. You can do all things and help me to do all You want me to do for You.

October 7

Jesus, the Prince of Peace. You are peace and You are in me. Let me have a peace that goes beyond anything my mind can comprehend. Please allow me to see things from Your perspective because that is what You can bring about in the storms of my life. You are near because You said You would never leave me. Let me walk close to You.

October 8

Jesus, the Lion of Judah, is how You have been described. You descended to us and ascended for us. You left, but You are still here. Fierceness brings about fear to the enemy. I ask that You help me tread over the enemy of death and destruction. You gave me life when my enemies didn't want me to live any longer. Help me fight the good fight and win this battle of life I face.

October 9

Jesus, I will stand before You one day to be judged. While I live, continue to intercede on my behalf. The Accuser wants me to see all I have done wrong. Help me this day to see what I am doing right. Intercede for me and disrupt what has been planned by the enemy. I want to see You now and see all the good that has been done on Your behalf.

October 10

Jesus, one day You are coming back. I want to be a part of Your kingdom that You will establish on earth. That's when I can experience peace on earth as it was meant from the beginning. You will always be and I always want to be with You. Abundant living is here in this life, and that is the life I want to live. Thank You for being with me forever more.

October 11

Jesus, You lived before You were born here and You continue to live after You left here. I want to have more life in my living. You showed me how to live and I want to live that way this day. I may not understand what is happening to me, but I know You not only know, but also understand. I'm not sure I will ever understand. The one thing I need to know is to know You as my Lord and Savior.

October 12

Jesus, life has more than one season and so does my personal life. I need You at all times and for all my life. Questions in life cause me to question You. You have no questions because You are the Answer. When I ask, please remind me that I will never have all the answers. I only need You and that will answer it all.

October 13

Jesus, when I call out Your name, will You call me by name? Let me know I am not just a sinner, but a saint. I want to be the one that would die for You if I were the only one living. Death is certain and life will someday come to an end. I want no regrets, but only You. Bring about a change today that will cause me to live for You more than ever before. I want to live for my Redeemer and die with no regrets.

October 14

Jesus, You seem so far away at times and yet You are only a whisper away. When I say Your name, I know things can change. I look for a better way to live a life that is not bitter. You chose me before I could even choose You. Help me to no longer see the road before me with detours, but one that was destined for more from the beginning. You are Lord and I want to serve You each day and sing praises to Your holy name. Thank You for being the world to me and choosing to come into my world.

October 15

Jesus, for so long I tried to live my life in a way that was pleasing to You. I know it must be lived in faith until I take my final breath. Faith, though, escapes me. It grows stronger and then it dissipates like vapor. It is nowhere around. I know it comes from within and is to be lived daily. I have unbelief and yet I need to believe in You and the promises You say are for those who truly believe. Today I make a decision to once again follow You. It may not be any easier, but I do know it is possible. I believe it because I believe in You.

October 16

Jesus, I look over the vastness of this land and wonder, "Why me?" Why did You place this calling on my life? With a calling also comes a cross. It's more than I can take at times, yet on Your cross You bore all our sins. I accept this calling, even with the questions that go along with it. I am precious in Your sight. Please see me through so I can say in the end, "You were there all the time."

October 17

Jesus, You are so precious to me. I want to live for You because of the way you not only lived, but also how You died for me. You knew when death was approaching. I don't, or at least not yet. I don't know how long I have left, but I don't want to leave You out of anything or any day. Why miss out when so much is yet to come my way? I bless Your holy name. I want my life to be about You, the risen Savior, who conquered death and is coming again. I love You so much that I want to live for You so You can live through me.

October 18

Jesus, life comes from You, the One who had the life taken out of You by Your enemies. You lived so I can live. I want to be a faithful witness and follower. You know where I need to be and how I am to get there. I ask for protection along the way. I want to use what lessons I learned, both from my experiences and my mistakes. I don't want to make the same decisions that were not the best. Help me to give others insight about this journey called life. I want never want to lose sight of You or my mission.

October 19

Jesus, You asked Your followers, "Who do you say that I am?" In the end, they had to respond with their lives. At the end of my life, I will also have to give You my final answer. No one can answer for me and there will never be another opportunity. I know what I want to say, but I also must live it for my answer to be more than just mere words.

October 20

Jesus, I want those closest to me to see a close walk with You. I want them to be able to ask me how they can live the same life. My prayer is for them to see the difference You make. You changed me completely with a new life and a new ending that will come one day.

October 21

Jesus, I believe so many people want to believe in You, but have questions that roll into doubts. Some may look at my life and question if I really knew what I was doing when I decided to pursue You with a passion. You knew from the start I would make that decision. Help me to make my life end well and know You will be well pleased.

October 22

Jesus, You experienced unparalleled temptation during Your ministry on earth. Your mission and message were questioned.

You gave until there was nothing else left to give. I want to give My all for You and know the mission for me at the beginning of time was completed before life ended for me on earth. Let Your will be done in me before I take my final step and last breath.

October 23

Jesus, the condition of people will never change until we recognize the condition we are in. Our faith has not always persevered and we justify our sinful ways. You said things would get worse. Tribulation is upon us, yet very little movement has been made toward You. Help us to see our condition and still sense Your compassion for us. Extend Your hand of mercy and withhold Your judgment. We must fall on our faces before You or lose what we were blessed with from You.

October 24

Jesus, Your grace has brought me through so many difficult situations. There were times when I didn't know if You really existed. But when it was over, I could see You were there all the time. You brought me through and I believe You will do the same again for me as I face another dilemma. Help me make it through this time of uncertainty and be sensitive to what You are doing.

October 25

Jesus, the equipping for the calling is still within me. I want those talents to be used to their fullest while I am living this life on earth. If I don't use them, it's as if I buried them, just like the parable of the hidden talents. Have me in the place where I am used the most for the work of Your kingdom on earth. Nothing will be hidden anymore. I want to be all for You with all that I have from You.

October 26

Jesus, make me a channel where You bless others and bring revelation to their world. You speak and live through Your servants. I humbly ask that You help me become that beacon of hope that shines into this dark world. Drive the darkness of depression and discouragement out of me. Replace it with the light of Your words and Your love. Bring peace, even when I don't understand why there seems to be nothing on the horizon. When I get there, I know You will already be there.

October 27

Jesus, all the strength I need today can come from You. Help me to draw on it and not falter when strength is needed. I sometimes fight battles my own way and come out defeated. No adversary can overcome me if I rely on You to help me be an over comer.

October 28

Jesus, there are some who don't want to live a day without knowing Your presence is with them. Others never acknowledge who You are and what can be done in Your name. I want to be one that knows You in a personal way and draws upon the strength that comes through You. Make this day one of joy and victory.

October 29

Jesus, You know what tomorrow holds. Prepare me to face whatever it might be. You wouldn't send something my way if I could not make it in Your strength. Shield my mind from the darts of the enemy. Provide me emotional stability to stand firm for You and not allow me to lose what You entrusted to me.

October 30

Jesus, on the day You called me to be a part of the family of God, I accepted You into my life. I know You never left me nor will I ever be without Your presence. Help me to not only know, but to also sense it. When I tell others about You, may they be overwhelmed by what You can also do for them. May my actions be even louder than my words. I not only want to tell others about You, but also show them what a difference You made in my life.

October 31

Jesus, the strength You demonstrated to stand against evil is a living example of how life is to be lived. Every day brings on a new battle for the mind. I want to have Your mind, the mind of Christ. Let me face each day with a renewed mind and renewed strength. I can't make it on yesterday's victories, but on the strength I draw daily from You.

November 1

Jesus, I see fellow believers following into traps cleverly set by the enemy. Their actions have been justified in their minds. Their testimonies diminish as they defend why such actions were taken. I can lose all that I stand for in a moment. I want to guard against evil schemes sometime conjured up in my mind that give me a pass to move ahead with selfish motives. That can never be from You, so help me not to ever let it come to pass.

November 2

Jesus, light my world of darkness with a tender love and guiding light to move me out of this current dilemma. I know what I am thinking is not from You. How I feel is not something You want me to experience. Guide me to the harbor of safety where I can rest my weary mind and tired body.

November 3

Jesus, life is worth living when I sense You are living in and through me. Just the mention of Your name by others who experience You in their lives bring hope. Thank You for the Holy Spirit that was sent when You left this earth. You knew what we would be facing and also when we could not make it alone. Bring comfort where I hurt the most and compassion to my helplessness.

November 4

Jesus, I know life is more than just confessing Your name. It's professing a belief in You and recognizing who You are. A mortal man could not have died for the sins of others. You are the Savior who took on the form of a mortal man but rose from the grave and ascended on high. Help me to remember that You, who conquered death and the grave, sit at the right hand of the God of heaven and earth.

November 5

Jesus, You showed compassion and also courage. There are times when I feel like hiding. Sometimes I fail to extend compassion to those who really need Your touch. Help me to be sensitive and yet strong. Give me the strength to not waver when I know I am to make a stand. Show me what You would do and then I want to act accordingly.

November 6

Jesus, Your disciples gave up all to follow You. I sometimes put too much emphasis on things that are of little value when compared to the benefit of selling out completely to You. Help is what I need, so help me to have the faith that is needed. You've never failed me yet and I must always remember that in the future.

November 7

Jesus, help me to see what You want me to see. I have tunnel vision and get locked into it at times without seeing the big picture. Life is more than just about my world. It's the world around me that must be seen. Let me see life through Your eyes and help those who need to feel Your compassion.

November 8

Jesus, the road seems to be more winding as I make this journey called life. I don't know what is ahead and don't fully understand where it is taking me. I want to see You at the journey's end with outstretched arms saying, "Welcome home, My child."

November 9

Jesus, I see those who seldom acknowledge Your presence in their lives and yet are successful by claiming to make it on their own. It's not about success, but about servant hood. Life is not measured just in terms of riches, but by living in the richness of Your presence. Send me to the place where I can be a blessing to those who need You the most.

November 10

Jesus, when asked to share what You mean to me, it's hard to explain if others don't know You. It's Your love that draws one close to You. It's Your strength that gives us the ability to fight the good fight. I can't really explain You. One must experience You in order to know You more than just head knowledge. It's a Spirit to spirit connection that is needed to have a better understanding, to know You in a more personal way.

November 11

Jesus, there is a beauty and calmness to those who choose to stay close by Your side. They know You can be all things at all times. You are not here just to fulfill our wishes, but for us to be filled with Your love and compassion. You never gathered a following by promising prosperity and position. You talked about a cross and having nowhere to lay Your head. Less can sometimes be more fulfilling. You know what I need and I know my needs will be supplied according to Your riches in glory.

November 12

Jesus, when the day comes that I lay down my cross, I want it to be in Your timing and not mine. Almost daily I want to bear it no more, but there is more of life left to live. Anything less is an incomplete life. Help me bear this cross completely to the end, knowing it will never have to be carried again.

November 13

Jesus, there are times when I know You are close to me. At other times, I don't sense Your presence, even though You are with me. Let me feel the gentleness of Your touch and sense the stillness of Your presence. Comfort me and calm me. Strengthen me and show me. Touch my mind and make my heart tender. For others to see You in me, I must first sense Your presence in me. I want to be all about You and nothing else. Be with me as I do Your kingdom work on earth.

November 14

Jesus, I fail at some things in life, but I know I am not a failure with You living inside of me. Those closest to You made mistakes while You were in their presence. I made my share and will make more, but that doesn't mean You love me less. Your love is unchangeable and unfaltering. Let me have an unfailing love and an undying loyalty for You.

November 15

Jesus, the way life is being lived today seems to seldom acknowledge You. Your name is hardly called out unless there is a crisis. You deserve more recognition than when one needs to be rescued. You deserve praise. I want You to be ever present in my mind and to know I am always in Your presence.

November 16

Jesus, my walk with You is not what I want it to be. I took baby steps when I learned to walk. I also took small steps when I became a follower of You. Sometimes I now stumble. I may even falter. Someone who loved me when I was a child picked me up. I am one of Yours and know You are there to lift me up. Hold me as I gain my confidence. Hold my hand as I regain my strength. Help me make it to the other side as my journey ends.

November 17

Jesus, I want to inspire and encourage others who are discouraged and downtrodden. When no one was there to help, I had a sense of hopelessness. No one knows who needs help and how to help more than You. Let that be part of me. I want to impart Your love and compassion, but I must first accept them from You. The enemy reminds me I am not deserving, but Your desire for me is to experience You fully and to live fully alive in Your presence.

November 18

Jesus, You became the Redeemer of mankind. You brought us out of a hopeless world to a life of hope. You gave us a reason to live. You showed us how to live abundantly. You said You will come again for us. I want to live a life that has little regret, a big heart for You and be a blessing to the kingdom.

November 19

Jesus, the mention of Your name causes me to think of Your love for me. How could You love me so much when I have given You so little in return? You gave me a reason to live. You know what You want me to be for You. Give me clarity and confidence going forward. I know of no one I want to please anymore than You.

November 20

Jesus, You died for me before I ever lived. You knew me before I ever knew You. How could You love someone under those conditions? You chose to do so and I am thankful You made that decision. I will never forget what You did for me and I need to always be mindful of what I can do for You.

November 21

Jesus, the way of the cross is what leads me home. It was the means that returned You to Your Father. I bear a cross daily. I sometimes wonder if it is worth the difficulties it brings in my life. If it takes me home and into the loving arms of a heavenly Father, then all will be worth it. Help me this day to feel more than the pain of the cross. Allow me to know Your presence while bearing it.

November 22

Jesus, the stone was rolled back from the tomb. It wasn't to let You out, but to let us in and see the miracle You experienced. I ask You to help me experience more than darkness and emptiness. Let others look into my life and see the miracle You brought to me that can become light to their lives. I want that same resurrection power to change me now and forever more.

November 23

Jesus, I so much want a change in my life. I need for You to touch me where I am this moment. I can't go any farther without You holding my hand and leading me to a better place than where I am now. It may be a slow move by You, but at least let me know something is taking place. If I remain in one place, I feel as if I am sinking. Rescue me. Restore me and place me on solid ground.

November 24

Jesus, I tell others the good news about how my life changed for You. I feel as if it has changed very little anymore. I become fearful when I don't sense Your presence. I lose faith when I don't see a move of You in my present condition. Let me know You are with me, even if it is just a shadow I faintly recognize. Touch me again. Let me know You love me. Help me remove all those clouds of discouragement from my mind and doubts that linger on the horizon.

November 25

Jesus, I talk about you, but I need to do more than just talk. I need less doubt. They fill my thoughts which cause me to have less faith. Faith brings about miracles. I want to believe more so I can have more faith. And I know that will bring about more miracles that are much needed for this moment in my life.

November 26

Jesus, when I am left alone, I know You didn't leave me. You told me that You are here. I read it in the Word. I choose to believe it. I know if I believe, I will experience it. Be with me. Be near me. Be a part of me now. I need You more than ever before.

November 27

Jesus, help me to be ready to do Your will and go to any destination You want me to follow You. Lead me into Your righteousness. Place me where others will see You in me. I prefer light, but You said to be a light in this world. I must be around those who experience darkness for Your light to be seen in me. Let me be a light that lights the way to You. Thank You for those You placed along my journey that helped lead me out of darkness and dark valleys.

November 28

Jesus, I believed You with childlike faith. I know we are to mature, but still be able to simply believe. Some things take greater faith and the way it becomes limited is by the way I believe. I want to see more of You and You ask that I show You more faith. Help me to see You all around me and all that You are doing in my life. Discouragement can turn into encouragement when I choose to see life from Your perspective. You desire the best for me and I want that for myself also. You called it abundant living. That's the life where You can give me the desires of my heart.

November 29

Jesus, how did You make it through when You knew what it would be like before You ever began? You were aware of the opposition before anyone ever opposed You. Herod came against You upon Your arrival on earth. People still oppose You, even when You are no longer here. The enemy knows me and opposes me. I want to stay on course as You direct my steps. Take me where I need to go. Lead me all the way. I will be opposed as I go, but I know You will lead me home where I belong when this life is over.

November 30

Jesus, much has been lost along the way. I gave up much in order to follow You. I laid down dreams and ambitions. I thought more rewards would have been experienced along the way. Yet what I see as things lost were never to be a part of me. You know what is best, along with the how and when to bring it about. You gave Your best and what You still have for me is nothing less. I will continue to look for the best and look for ways I can best serve You.

December 1

Jesus, there are people in my life who measure success by their own standards. That's not the way I want to be measured. You told us how to live. You demonstrated it. And now we have Your power to live that way. Help me not to make life an act of labor, but one of love. You loved others. You loved Your enemies enough to die for them. I want to live fully alive and full of Your love. That's life worth living.

December 2

Jesus, I can only go through You to the place You want me to go. I would not know if You had not made it known. You chose to do so and now I choose to follow You. Show me the way to live. I want my life to be about showing others. I look for the opportunity to express Your love to others. I choose to be hopeful so others can see there is hope in You, my blessed hope.

December 3

Jesus, I am instructed in the Bible to have Your mind, the mind of Christ. Your thinking helped You make it through this life. I may feel like my life is not making much difference because I don't see all that can be seen. There is a spiritual realm that I sometimes forget exists. I know there are more of the fiery darts that didn't hit me than the ones who found me as the target. Thank You for being my shield and for the hedge You have around me. Guard my mind and my body from the damage the enemy wants to inflict upon me. Thank You for keeping me safe all the way home.

December 4

Jesus, be my Shield that brings safety. Be the hedge of protection that keeps the enemy at bay. They may see me, but don't let them touch me. Keep me from becoming fearful that may cause them to close in on me. I will not be hurt. I will not be disgraced. Keep my eyes on You and Your presence. No longer will I be an easy prey. That is my prayer.

December 5

Jesus, You are my shield. I need protection as I try to get my footing on solid ground. Thank You for protecting me from the fiery darts that missed their targets. Thank You also for bringing healing when I became wounded. Your wounds opened the way for me to experience You in a way I never knew before.

December 6

Jesus, You said the way to You is narrow. Sometimes it becomes so narrow that I don't know if I am on the right road. Very few seem to want to travel this way. Doubts cloud the mind as darkness makes the direction impossible to determine. Light my way with Your presence. Show me the way by Your gentle nudge. Thank You for bringing me this far. Thank You for leading me home.

December 7

Jesus, I hear people say they know what is best for me. They base their knowledge on what they've known in the past. But that doesn't guarantee safe passage into the days ahead. They may know where they came from, but don't know where You want me to go. Only You know the way because You said, "I am the way." You went ahead of me. That makes You know the way. Be with me like You have been all along. Then I will have nothing to fear.

December 8

Jesus, You exchanged Your stripes for my chains. You gave me Your all while the enemy tries to take it all away from me. I want to live the way You want me to live each day. Help me to make it one that counts the most for You. You never gave up while living. I want to live for You, even while dying.

December 9

Jesus, no one cares for me like You. I may not do or say things that You approve, but You never abandon me. My words may hurt others, but Your discipline doesn't destroy me. Your patience never runs out because of Your undying love for me. You never regretted what You did for me. Help me to live the remainder of my life that will have less regrets than I do now.

December 10

Jesus, I think about things I am unable to share with others. I dread some things that never come to pass. I worry about events that really don't matter in the long run. Worry, fear, and anxiety have never worked to my advantage. In the end, You are all that matters. What You think about me brings joy and a sense of hope. You loved me before I knew You. And You still love me even though You know all there is to be know about me.

December 11

Jesus, I concern myself with what others think about me, but don't give enough thought how You want me to live for You. I am Your witness, Your disciple, Your follower, and part of the family of God. I want to be the one that makes You glad. You chose me. I want You to be able to point to me at any moment and say, "That's a follower of Mine that I want others to follow." And I want to always point others to You.

December 12

Jesus, the love I have for You is sometimes how I think You see me. If I am not very pleasing, then I believe You are not pleased with me. But You know my heart. You know how I truly think and feel about You. I want to be in love with You so that nothing will ever change that love. Thank You for not giving up on me or changing the way You love me.

December 13

Jesus, there are times when I wonder how I missed out on things I thought would be coming to me in life from You. It affects my view of life about You since there is less time for You to fulfill all I believe You promised me. Help me not to be left out because I have less faith. It's sometimes so hard to believe when I don't see anything happening in that area. But I will still believe You have the best for me that is still yet to come.

December 14

Jesus, You kept all Your promises. Some have been made known in very convincing and clear ways. Others were revealed in more subtle and unassuming ways. Thank You for all those times when I never knew it was You. Give me the strength not to give up as my life has less years to live than before. You kept Your word and I want to keep the promises I made in earnest and with sincerity. I do love You, regardless of how unlovely I became when I thought You broke a promise to me.

December 15

Jesus, some people today believe things I used to believe, but now I'm not sure if I believe what I did earlier. Years of struggles sometime slowly wear away what beliefs I considered a strong foundation. But I know faith is the cornerstone of moving forward. I want the rock solid faith like I had when I became a believer. You never change and I want to be an unshakable and immovable force for Your kingdom on earth.

December 16

Jesus, I see those who have a look of hopelessness in their eyes. They need to be reassured that in the end You will be victorious. I must have hope in order to share hope. Help me to see all the good things because of You being in my life. You died for me and I want to live for You in a way so others want to live for You also.

December 17

Jesus, when things were more simple in life, faith seemed to be more simple. As life becomes more complex, my simple faith doesn't seem to be sufficient. Yet You said one only needs faith the size of a mustard seed. Take what I have and multiply it, like You did the loaves of bread, that will help others.

December 18

Jesus, I see You from one perspective while others may see You from another. I base my ways and my view of life upon that perspective. I know You are a multi-faceted God and no one will ever know all Your ways. Let me see You the way You desire to be seen. Help me to experience Your grace when it is needed in my life. Let me experience discipline in a way that can only come as a result of Your love for me. Show me how I can be more like You.

December 19

Jesus, the faith of my spiritual fathers on earth gave me hope. They believed in You and believed Your Son. I want to have the same faith in my heavenly Father, like they did in Him. Believe. I must simply believe. More belief means I will have less unbelief. Let me see something that I can hang on to until my feet find more solid ground.

December 20

Jesus, there will never be a dilemma I'm experiencing that You will be unable to help me through if I believe in You. You are with me in the deepest of valleys. I will never be alone, for You are with me. If You choose to be silent in those valleys, let me sense Your presence. Let Your presence be louder than what You would speak into my spirit. I want to hear from You, but I need to know You are with me this moment.

December 21

Jesus, I want the remaining days of my life to be different than ever before. Allow me to rest in Your presence. I don't want to strive or worry about the future anymore. I must not fear the future or live in the past. As I move into tomorrow, I do so with anticipation. I look for You in all things that come my way. I know You will be my provider. Thank You for the bread today. I know tomorrow will take care of itself.

December 22

Jesus, the way seems long and looks to be longer each day. But You know when the end will come and where I will be at that time. I gave You my life and my future. The past is gone and the future is yet to arrive. Today is what I can offer You. I want to make it the best and know You will be pleased.

December 23

Jesus, the turns and curves in life come up rather quickly. They are unseen until I see my life going in different directions. I don't know what is facing me until I come face to face with that situation. I ask for Your presence to be felt and Your purpose to be made known. I love You. Help me to have the trust in You that You desire from me. No one can take better care of me than You. I am trying to trust You with all that is in me. Please accept it and help me to know You still have even greater things ahead.

December 24

Jesus, the day will arrive when I face death closer than ever before. I know the enemy wants me dead. I want to live until I've squeezed the last ounce of living out of life. I don't want to leave any unfulfilled dreams behind. I don't want to have any talents that were left hidden inside of me. Let the day be a positive one that allows me to experience Your will and feel Your presence as never before.

December 25

Jesus, this is the day most people think about You, but many are doing it less and less. That doesn't diminish the sacredness of the day. We don't always think about where we would be without You being born as one of us. I want to have more of a part in Your kingdom work here on earth. You gave me life. Now I want to give You more of my life than ever before. Your death brought me life. Help me to make my life all about You until the day I have no more life in me.

December 26

Jesus, the life I live is with You in mind. I think about what needs to be eliminated that may keep You from revealing more of Your truths to me. Let my words come directly from You as I interact with those I come in contact with today. May I have Your Spirit resting on me like You experienced when making this journey in life.

December 27

Jesus, my words sometime cause people to become confused. I tell them how I trust You, but then it is followed by words of doubt and a lack of confidence in You. Help me to close the door of my mind on negative thinking and close my mouth to words that speak doubt and discouragement. I choose to speak words of life and think thoughts of hope. Lift my hopelessness to the level of certainty where Your promises will be fulfilled in my lifetime.

December 28

Jesus, some thoughts that are conjured up in my mind seem to come out of nowhere. They are things I don't want to dwell on or even entertain for a moment. Help me to ask for Your mind at that time and know You want me to dwell on Your thoughts. Keep me pure in my walk with You and that my thoughts will come from You. I don't want to be a part of this world in my thoughts, but dwell on those things that are pure and holy. Make my a vessel of praise and purity so that others can see You and nothing of me.

December 29

Jesus, there are days when I don't know if I can make it even halfway through the day. But somehow I make it. It's because of

Your grace and mercy toward me that You still have a reason for my existence on earth. I want to fulfill Your plan that was set in motion in the beginning and to complete life, knowing the race was run well. Touch my mind today and make it one of confidence and consistency. Place the words on my lips that give encouragement to others and lift Your name on high. You are the Messiah and the King of Kings. I am Your servant in waiting and willing to be used by You in a way I never dreamed possible this side of heaven.

December 30

Jesus, I see many of my friends get caught in the web of deception and defeat that was spun by the enemy. They never thought it would happen to them, but sadly, it did. I say I would never be caught in that dilemma, but I have never been in their situation. Help me to better understand and be more forgiving of their wrongdoing. I hope they would reach out to me and not abandon me if I was in their position. Let them know there is no sin or wrongdoing so great that Your blood doesn't cover. Thank You for that kind of love for us.

December 31

Jesus, You helped me make it through another year. There were some celebrations, but some deep hurt and heartaches along the way. I know I am not promised another year, even another day. But if I rise up tomorrow to another day given by You, I want to make the best of it. I want to make the best of this upcoming year, regardless of how long or short it may be. Let it be one that I can hear You say, "It was the best one yet lived for Me." Amen.